D1572580

Best Regards
Evan F. Kolil

The Man Who Wouldn't Kill Cats

The Story of Evan Kalik
as told to
David Michael Smith

PORTLAND • OREGON
INKWATERPRESS.COM

Scan this QR Code to
learn more about this title

4theLoveofCats.com

All proceeds from there sale of this book go to support the Cat Alliance Team Sanctuary (CATS) and are tax deductible.

Cover and interior layout by Masha Shubin
Cover design by Sam Downey

Smith, David Michael, 1947-
       The man who wouldn't kill cats : the Evan Kalik story
   as told to David Michael Smith / David Michael Smith.
       pages cm
       LCCN 2013943318
       ISBN 978-1-59299-970-5 (hc)
       ISBN 978-1-59299-971-2 (e-book)

    1. Kalik, Evan. 2. Animal rights activists--United
States--Biography. 3. Animal welfare--United States--
Societies, etc. 4. Cat rescue--United States. 5. Cat
adoption--United States.   I. Kalik, Evan. II. Title.

    HV4764.S65 2013   179'.3'092
                                 QBI13-600145

Publisher: Inkwater Press | www.inkwaterpress.com

Hardback ISBN-13 978-1-59299-970-5 | ISBN-10 1-59299-970-0
Kindle ISBN-13 978-1-59299-971-2 | ISBN-10 1-59299-971-9

Printed in the U.S.A.
All paper is acid free and meets all ANSI standards for archival quality paper.

1 3 5 7 9 10 8 6 4 2

"*Thou art the Great Cat, the avenger of the Gods, and the judge of worlds, and the president of the sovereign chiefs and the governor of the holy Circle; thou art indeed the Great Cat.*"

INSCRIPTION ON THE ROYAL TOMBS AT THEBES

All proceeds from the sale of this book go to support the Cat Alliance Team Sanctuary

Table of Contents

Preface

WHEN A VETERINARIAN HEARS THE TITLE OF THIS BOOK, SHE OR HE IS LIKELY to recoil with concern. In conversations with animal doctors I have, in fact, witnessed the near apoplexy with which the words "cats" and "killed" are used in the same sentence. The reason is because of the strength gained over the past couple of decades of the "no kill" animal shelter movement. Even the hint of suggestion that animals are euthanized has become taboo. At least in some instances. This is a good thing, regardless of how nuanced is the topic of non-human animal euthanasia.

Unfortunately, the primary strategy for dealing with domesticated animals that have behavioral issues, illnesses, or are simply unwanted is euthanasia. It is the resistance to that strategy that makes the stories of Evan Kalik and his collaborators so compelling. He, and some like him, simply will not kill cats. Read on to find out why they think there are other solutions besides snuffing out the lives of millions of animals every year that we human animals find "inconvenient."

One of my earliest memories is getting the tip of one of my thumbs bitten off by an aggressive squirrel. It wasn't anybody's fault, especially the squirrel's. I wanted to feed him and he simply mistook the tip of my appendage as a part of the bread I was holding. It hurt, but I remember being more fascinated by getting that close to a wild animal than overwhelmed by pain.

My sister, Gina, and I both received the gift of having animals as part of our lives from our dad. Not too far down the road from the biting incident, a rainstorm washed a baby squirrel out of its nest and Dad rescued her. Suzie lived in the pocket of his shirt for almost two years before she contracted some mysterious illness and died. An understanding of death as part of life came with each of the animals we had as companions through the years. There was a pet cemetery in our back yard, filled with the bones of various squirrels, dogs, cats, rabbits, and birds. Dad was never mawkish about it. Rather, it was a way of honoring our little pals and giving them a proper send send-off to beyond the beyond.

In the before time of my childhood in the 1950s, when "recycle" meant running your washing through the machine again, my dad and I visited the city dump, as it was unceremoniously called, to drop off the biweekly accumulation of life's detritus from around our house. On one such visit, Dad allowed me to take along a pump action .22-caliber rifle bequeathed to him by his maternal grandfather. I was no more than eight or nine years old and had seen enough Westerns to want to shoot and kill something. There standing amongst the mounds of garbage stood a bird – I don't recall what kind – minding its own business as it went about surviving by pecking through man's decompositions. I shot him right through the middle of his tiny body, really for no other reason that to see what it would feel like. It felt terrible. As I stood over the failing bird, a hole clearly visible with droplets of red blood oozing forth, I watched as the small avian took a final breath or two and then died. I remember vividly that I swore to myself I would never do such a thing again. I also recall vowing to the bird's puny corpse that somehow I would take this lesson with me so that its life would not have been taken in vain. I only wish, fifty-plus years later, that I could have read this moral tale in a book rather than having actualized it. Some of life's most poignant lessons are like that. One must have the actual experience in order to really learn what it is that Nature wishes to teach us. This lesson has never been forgotten or repeated and perhaps, in small measure, I have been able to atone for it.

My bird slaying diversion aside, the result of all my childhood focus on animal companions is that I cannot recall any stage of my life where there hasn't been something with four legs or fins running through my existence. For the past few decades, I have honed a lot of my attention on legless aquatic life. When the oceans are gone, we won't be far behind their demise. Thus have I sailed with Paul Watson of the Sea Shepherd Conservation Society into Russian Siberian waters to help draw attention to the slaughter of California Gray Whales. I have also worked closely with Sea Watch, a non-profit group dedicated to revitalizing the Sea of Cortez. Whatever my activities on behalf of whatever species, always in the background have been my beloved cats (and very often dogs, as well).

There are countless rescue stories I could share, tales of animal frivolity – in and out of the oceans – and moments of agonizing sorrow at the
loss of one animal friend or another. My energies lie now in helping spread
the word about Evan Kalik so that others can learn from his successes and
readily admitted shortcomings. It is our intention to create a clear picture
of every element that goes into the creation of an organized effort to direct
one's attention to the saving of non-human animal life. We believe that
communities across the country – perhaps the world – could benefit from
the blueprints already made and executed by Evan. The level of suffering
among the cat populations of our world is completely unacceptable. With
perseverance, tenacity, courage, vision, and (yes, here it comes…) money,
there is no reason why countless other communities could not achieve some
measure of the victories accrued by Evan and the people he has inspired.

My first meeting with Evan Kalik was during a formal videotaped interview session. My first impression of him was probably not unlike that of
everyone who first meets him. Like an elderly Whirling Dervish, he flits
about with the energy of a man half his age. Filled with anecdotes that range
from his early dream of opening a shelter right up until the present day, he
is at once engaging, charming, and a bit overwhelming. When he discovers
that you share at least a little of his passion for cats and other non-human
animals, you are on the road to a beautiful friendship.

If you think that perhaps euthanasia is an answer to too many cats in
the world (which I emphatically do not) then watch out! Evan Kalik will
recalibrate your thinking straight away. As you will learn in these pages,
Evan will not abide by taking a cat's life except under the most dire circumstances, those dictated by deep compassion and concern for the suffering of
a sentient being. Thus he is truly The Man Who Wouldn't Kill Cats.

Like eternity itself, cats are completely inscrutable, and I like it that
way. Call one and they won't usually come – because they know that's what
YOU want, and that doesn't count very much with a cat. The flip side of
that coin comes when a cat decides to take you on, whether for just a few
moments, or a lifetime. I have three cats in my life now, all of whom I think
of as my "puppy" cats. They follow me everywhere. I mean everywhere.
I can't even visit the bathroom without them wanting to join me. Every
morning, when I throw open the shower curtain after a morning's scrubbing,

there's boy cat, Brad, standing at attention, ready to provide instructions on just how I should towel off. If I stay up too late in the evening, one or more of the three are there to meow a reminder that it's time to hit the hay. They insist on my clearing a special spot for them on the sheet near my head. Yes, of course, I do it. They are cats, after all. I, a mere human.

When you witness enough synchronicity in your life, you abandon the idea of meaningless coincidence. Albert Einstein once observed:

> *There are two ways to live: you can live as if nothing is a miracle; you can live as if everything is a miracle.*

My selection is the latter, for there is an overabundance of the miraculous in my life every day. Cats are one of those miracles. Every time I run my hand along a cat's torso, look into a cat's eyes, or allow its purring to lull me into a trance, I am transported from the mundane to the marvelous. It has come time for me to give back to my little messengers from eternity. I do so with devotion and joy, and I thank Evan Kalik for allowing me this opportunity to be of some small service. Viva la Cats!

The Kitten and the Falling Leaves

That way look, my infant, lo!
What a pretty baby-show!
See the kitten on the wall,
sporting with the leaves that fall.
Withered leaves - one - two and three
from the lofty elder tree.
Though the calm and frosty air,
of this morning bright and fair.
Eddying round and round they sink,
softly, slowly; one might think.
From the motions that are made,
every little leaf conveyed
Sylph or Faery hither tending,
to this lower world descending.
Each invisible and mute,

in his wavering parachute.
But the Kitten, how she starts,
crouches, stretches, paws, and darts!
First at one, and then its fellow,
just as light and just as yellow.
There are many now - now one,
now they stop and there are none:
What intenseness of desire,
in her upward eye of fire!
With a tiger-leap half-way,
now she meets the coming prey.
lets it go as fast, and then;
Has it in her power again.
Now she works with three or four,
like an Indian conjuror;
quick as he in feats of art,
far beyond in joy of heart.
Where her antics played in the eye,
of a thousand standers-by,
clapping hands with shout and stare,
what would little Tabby care!
For the plaudits of the crowd?
Over happy to be proud,
over wealthy in the treasure
of her exceeding pleasure!

WILLIAM WORDSWORTH (1770–1850)

Animal Rights Timeline

THIS TIMELINE, REPRINTED WITH THE KIND PERMISSION OF ITS CREATOR, DORIS Lin, is by no means an exhaustive history, but is meant to give an overview of some of the major events in the modern animal rights movement.

Concern for animal suffering is not a new or modern idea. Many read the ancient Hindu and Buddhist scriptures as advocating a vegetarian diet for ethical reasons. The ideology has evolved continuously over millennia, but many animal activists point to the publication of *Animal Liberation* in 1975 in the United States as the catalyst for the modern American animal rights movement.

1975 – *Animal Liberation* by philosopher Peter Singer is published.

1979 – The Animal Legal Defense Fund is established.

1979 – The National Anti-Vivisection Society establishes World Lab Animal Day, on April 24. The day has evolved into World Laboratory Animal Week.

1980 – People for the Ethical Treatment of Animals (PETA) is founded.

1980 – *Animal Factories* by attorney Jim Mason and philosopher Peter Singer is published.

1981 – The Farm Animal Reform Movement is officially founded.

1983 – The Farm Animal Reform Movement establishes World Farm Animals Day on October 2.

1983 – *The Case for Animal Rights* by philosopher Tom Regan is published.

1985 – The first annual Great American Meatout is organized by Farm Animal Reform Movement.

1986 – Fur Free Friday, an annual nationwide fur protest on the day after Thanksgiving, begins.

1986 – Farm Sanctuary is founded.

1987 – California high school student Jennifer Graham makes national headlines when she refuses to dissect a frog.

1987 – *Diet for a New America* by John Robbins is published.

1989 – Avon stops testing their products on animals.

1989 – In Defense of Animals launches their campaign against Procter & Gamble's animal testing.

1990 – Revlon stops testing their products on animals.

1992 – The Animal Enterprise Protection Act passed.

1993 – General Motors stops using live animals in crash tests.

1993 – The Great Ape Project is founded.

1994 – Tyke the elephant goes on a rampage, killing her trainer and escaping from the circus before being gunned down by police.

1995 – Compassion Over Killing is founded.

1996 – Vegetarian activist and former cattle rancher Howard Lyman appears on Oprah Winfrey's talk show, leading to a defamation lawsuit filed by Texas Cattlemen.

1997 – PETA releases an undercover video showing animal abuse by Huntington Life Sciences.

1998 – A jury finds in favor of Lyman and Winfrey in the defamation lawsuit filed by Texas Cattlemen.

1998 – An investigation by The Humane Society of the U.S. reveals that Burlington Coat Factory is selling products made from dog and cat fur.

2001 – Compassion Over Killing conducts an open rescue at a battery hen facility, documenting abuses and rescuing eight hens.

2002 – *Dominion* by Matthew Scully is published.

2002 – McDonald's settles a class-action lawsuit over their non-vegetarian French fries.

2004 – Clothing chain Forever 21 promises to stop selling fur.

2005 – The U.S. Congress pulls funding for inspections of horse meat.

2006 – The "SHAC 7" are convicted under the Animal Enterprise Protection Act.

2006 – Animal Enterprise Terrorism Act is passed.

2006 – An investigation by the Humane Society of the U.S. reveals that items labeled as "faux" fur at Burlington Coat Factory are made of real fur.

2007 – Hayden Panettiere went to Japan and confronted Japanese fishermen that were killing dolphins. Due to her efforts she was awarded the Compassion in Action award from PETA.

Today – Many of the previously mentioned groups and organizations still remain. Many of the more recent groups that have formed over the past 10 years have been more wildlife related.[1]

---

1 Reprinted with permission of: Doris Lin http://animalrights.about.com/od/animalrights101/a/TimelineModern.htm

PART ONE

A Brief History of Man-Animal's Rights & Wrongs

"True benevolence, or compassion, extends itself through the whole of existence and sympathizes with the distress of every creature capable of sensation."

JOSEPH ADDISON

IT MAY NOT SEEM SO WHEN LOOKING ABOUT THE WORLD AT THE TERRIBLE INJUS-tices that have prevailed throughout the ages, but the truth is inexorable. Sooner or later, what is true moves to center stage, and the illusions that have blocked it from realization are removed. This is not merely a matter of faith. It is a Universal Law, the way things work. Perhaps Mahatma Gandhi said it best:

> *Truth is by nature self-evident. As soon as you remove the cobwebs of ignorance that surround it, it shines clear. When I despair, I remember that all through history the way of truth and love have always won. There have been tyrants and murderers, and for a time, they can seem invincible, but in the end, they always fall. Think of it — always.*

This axiom holds for the admittedly slow realization amongst human animals that their non-human animal companions on this planet have the same right to survive and flourish that men accord themselves. It has been, and continues to be, a long, twisted pathway to a planet-wide embracing of this simple truth, but progress is apparent all around us. The challenge is to not become discouraged by the unconscious, and often deliberate, cruelty and neglect to which so many non-human animals are still subjected.

According to psychologist Richard Ryder, former Mellon Professor at Tulane University and chairman of the Royal Society for the Preservation of Animals in 1977 (RSPCA), the first concern for the welfare of animals in Western civilization can be traced back to the Greeks in the 6th century BCE. Their philosophy of animism, as codified in the writings of Pythagoras (c. 580 – c. 500 BCE), viewed human and non-human animals alike as sharing the same kind of soul, a single spirit that permeates the entire universe, making us one with animals. Theophrastus (c. 371 – c. 287 BCE), a student of Aristotle, went so far as to assert that non-human animals enjoy the capacity to reason, making the idea of eating them preposterous in the extreme.

When it comes specifically to the cat, there is no other relationship on earth quite like the one between their species and ours. To be sure, we have long enjoyed a special bond with dogs, as well, but anyone who has studied the history of felines and their people know that cats have been reviled, loved, worshiped, and persecuted, depending on the time and place, like no other species.

Cats first allowed humans into their mysterious world during the Bronze Age and even late Stone Age in the Caucasus, Central Asia, and India. Cat remains have been excavated from archeological digs in all these locations, indicating that our ancestors liked having cats around the cave. About 5,000 years ago, that kinship really took a leap forward. It was a bit of a fluke that it happened at all. In a place then known as Upper Egypt, today called Sudan, a pragmatic relationship developed between our two species in the Valley of the Nile. Grain was the main staple of the Egyptian diet at that time, and rats enjoyed, as much as people, eating from the granaries where the precious food stuff was stored. Where there are rats there are cats, and soon enough the people of Egypt recognized that their little furry friends were keeping the rat population under control. This prompted people to cultivate a deeper relationship by leaving extra portions of this or that around for their four-legged food guardians to eat, to keep them interested enough to remain in the vicinity. The cats realized they had a good thing going, and soon there were plenty of them running about the country.

What really marked the beginning of the cat's ascension in status was the attention it received from the Pharaohs. The first Egyptian King, Menes, and subsequent Pharaohs, wanted as many cats as they could gather for themselves since the royal granaries were bursting with grain and drawing to them a corresponding army of hungry vermin. The trouble was, Egyptians had become quite attached to their kitties and it probably would have fomented a revolution had the royals simply confiscated all cats for their own use. Always a step ahead when it came to figuring out how to get what they wanted, the royals of Egypt elevated cats to the status of demi-gods. Not as important as the Pharaohs, of course, who fancied themselves divine, but still better than a mere ordinary human.

Thus were cats off to a sterling start in their affiliation with people. Should a house catch on fire in Egypt, it was the cats that were rescued first. Anyone fortunate enough to have a cat in their home was considered blessed. As long as the cat remained healthy, that is. Punishment was meted out to anyone unlucky enough to have a cat fall sick while under their care, and killing a cat was a capital crime, punishable by death. One of the local priests had to examine a cat when it died to make certain it did so of natural causes and not neglect. Social convention demanded that cats be properly grieved, with the homeowners shaving their eyebrows and beating their chests considered an appropriate expression of the loss. Just to prove how serious was the cat's status in ancient Egypt, a feline goddess called Bastet, or Bast, was worshiped from the Second Dynasty onward. Not every cat benefited from this elevated stature. More than 300,000 mummified cats were discovered when Bast's temple at Per-Bast was excavated.

Cats are also known to have enjoyed a comfortable standing with Romans during their days of empire. At least we know for certain no Roman ever mummified his or her cat. Cats came into the human story from early Russia and Ukraine, as well. In the formative days of Islam, cats were revered. Legend has it that the Prophet Mohammed adored cats enough to cut off the sleeve of his shirt that a cat was sleeping on, rather than disturb the cat during its nap. Now, *that* is a cat lover!

It was the cat's perennial rodent killing capabilities that contributed to its ongoing alliance with humankind. Felines were popular aboard ships for this reason, and their lineage spread rapidly around the globe. Following the example set by the Egyptians, other cultures thought enough of cats to also deify them. Freya, a Norse goddess during the Middle Ages, sported the body of a woman and the head of a cat. It was, in fact, the cat's place in so-called pagan religions that eventually led to its fall from grace. Christians, ever on the lookout for competing deities, decried cats as false gods and worse, associating them with the Inferior Force, namely Satan himself.

Somehow, the cat managed to hang on. Living far from his home in the 9th century in an attempt to avoid pillaging Norsemen, an Irish monk residing in Reichenau on Lake Constance found solace in his feline friend, Pangur Ban.

> I and Pangur Ban my cat,
> 'Tis a like task we are at,
> Hunting mice is his delight,
> Hunting words I sit all night.
>
> 'Tis a merry thing to see,
> At our tasks how glad are we
> When at home we sit and find,
> Entertainment to our mind.
>
> 'Gainst the wall he sets his eye,
> Full and fierce and sharp and sly,
> 'Gainst the wall of knowledge I,
> All my little wisdom try.
>
> So in peace our task we ply:
> Pangur Ban my cat and I
> In our arts and in our bliss,
> I have mine and he has his.

As the faith took hold in Medieval Europe, cats were tortured and burned alive as consorts of the devil. The consequence of their systematic persecution by the Church was dramatic. Cat populations were greatly depleted during this period, almost disappearing completely by 1400 CE. It is such shortsightedness that may have contributed heavily to the spread of the Plague, since there were few cats left to keep the rat population from carrying the deadly disease throughout the European continent. History seems to favor irony.

The Chinese weren't about to miss out on all the fun, and cats were common there by 500 BCE. As in the West, they began their odyssey as the strict purview of emperors and other royals, but soon enough made their way into the hearts and hearths of the common folks. Interbreeding gave birth to some of the varieties of cats we know today, as Persians from Persia, Siamese from Siam, Burmese from Burma, Bobtails from Japan, and Angoras from Turkey mingled with local wild cats.

One Japanese legend has it that a cat once stood in front of the Gotokuji Temple in Tokyo, beckoning passersby with its raised paw to come in. As a result, the story goes, the temple became wealthy. Worshipers are said to still attend this temple to pray for good fortune – for themselves and their cats. Statue representations of the "Beckoning Cat" are on display in some Japanese homes and businesses as good luck symbols.

Fast forward to the 17th century, when one of the most miserable events in history for cats came during the Salem, Massachusetts, witchcraft trials in the late 1600s. Women purported to be witches were hanged, along with their alleged feline familiars in the Dark Arts. The familiar's job was supposedly to report back to the devil about how all the witches' misdeeds were progressing.

The first animal protection legislation in the English-speaking world passed in 1635 in Ireland. In a reference to "cruelty used to beasts," the law prohibited attaching horses' tails to ploughs, as well as pulling wool off sheep. In 1641, the Massachusetts Bay Colony passed the first legal code in North America to protect domestic animals. Their constitution used *The Body of Liberties* by Puritan clergyman and lawyer Nathaniel Ward to guide them during creation of the code. In Ward's word, rite 92 asserted that "No man shall exercise any Tirrany or Crueltie toward any bruite Creature which are usuallie kept for man's use." It is interesting to note that this idea stands in stark juxtaposition to the idea espoused by French philosopher René Descartes in Europe at the time. He saw animals as mere automata. This meant that non-human animals, in Descartes' view, are complex organic machines, all of whose actions can be fully explained without any reference to the operation of mind or feeling.

Thanks to the Puritans, Descartes' ideas did not prevail everywhere in Europe at that time. In England, Oliver Cromwell's government passed animal protection legislation at the urging of the Puritans in 1654. Cromwell had a personal aversion to many popular "sports" of the day, including bull baiting, dog fighting, cock throwing, and cockfighting. The Puritans of the 17th century interpreted the bible in much the same manner as some modern-day Christians are beginning to do – that man's dominion over non-human animals means responsible stewardship rather than the ownership of property. Some people apparently cannot live without their blood sports, and these protections were overturned in 1660 when Charles II assumed the throne of England during a period known as the Restoration.

Unfortunately for generations of non-human animals of a wide range of species, the philosophical ideas of René Descartes were dominant in England and North America well into the 20th century. For Descartes, mind was separate from the physical universe, therefore condemning non-human animals to the realm of relative unconsciousness. Without consciousness, so the logic went, animals are incapable of feeling – suffering – so there was nothing cruel or unusual about treating animals in the same way a man would treat any other piece of property.

At the other end of the philosophical spectrum, John Locke (1632–1704 CE) argued in 1693 in his work *Some Thoughts Concerning Education* that "the custom of tormenting and killing of beasts will, by degrees, harden their minds even towards men" as a reason children should not mistreat non-human animals. He reasoned further that it was morally wrong for any human, adult or child, to exercise cruelty toward animals.

By the 18th century, with the Dark Ages behind them, members of the Felidae family had once again ascended to their rightful place in the human heart around the world. It would still be a long road ahead for cats and other non-human animals, however, in terms of humanity's capacity to accept their fellow creatures as sentient beings deserving of respect and kindness. David Walls, Professor Emeritus of Sociology at Sonoma State University, sees a rise in consciousness in humanity's relationship to other animals as paralleling our awakening to rights within the human community, such as the anti-slavery movement and later the movement for women's suffrage. In England, Parliament passed a bill intended to end bull-baiting in 1800. Horses and cattle came in for consideration in 1822 when the House of

Commons passed a bill to prevent cruelty to these domestic creatures. The bill's sponsor, Colonel Richard Martin, organized the Society for the Prevention of Cruelty to Animals (SPCA) two years later. The idea behind his organization gained enough prominence by 1840 that Queen Victoria decreed that the SPCA was to become the Royal Society for Prevention of Cruelty to Animals. The American SPCA was founded in New York in 1866, but remained primarily a local animal shelter program for several years.

By the late 1860s, according to Professor Walls, other SPCAs and Humane Societies were formed around the United States, with the support of abolitionists. Groups sprang up in Pennsylvania, Massachusetts, and San Francisco. In 1877, with an eye toward both human child welfare and animal care, the American Humane Association (AHA) was founded. As advances in human medicine developed, resistance against using animals in laboratory experiments took hold, fueled by the obvious suffering inflicted on animals in the years before anesthetics. According to Walls:

The anti-vivisection movement was strong in England and the United States in the 1890s (the American Anti-Vivisection Society was formed in Philadelphia in 1883), but was overwhelmed by the prestige of scientific medicine by the early twentieth century. The humane movement focused more on dogs and cats as the use of horses as beasts of burden declined and the keeping of pets increased. The center of action shifted to protection of wild animals and birds, as undertaken by the Audubon Societies founded in the late 1890s.

With the end of World War II, cats and dogs became an increasingly common adjunct to middle class households in the industrialized nations. It is estimated that a pet is present in 43% of U.S. households today, with somewhere between 51 and 58 million dogs spread across the nation, with roughly 49 to 60 million cats taking their place in the household.

Perhaps the most common critter amongst today's domestic cat is the Tabby, believed to have evolved from the African wild cat because of its markings. But the list of breeds today is long and varied, and there is a cat "look" and temperament for just about any human longing. Unfortunately, some breeds of cat (like Persians) are bred according to human preferences regardless of the hardships such breeding imposes on the cats. (Persians have difficulty breathing due to their distinctive lack of a nose with adequate nasal passages. Their eyes secrete excessively, as well.)

What is it about cats that arouses the loving passions of cat lovers the world over? There are probably as many answers to that question as there are people offering a reply, yet certain characteristics seem to boast a universal appeal. You would have to have a heart made of stone to resist the charms of newborn kittens. Regardless of the breed, first and foremost, cats are essentially mysterious. Their demeanor implies deep recesses of enigma and wonder. And those hypnotizing eyes! Their playfulness is matched only by their quietude, as the average cat sleeps eighteen hours a day, then bursts into explosions of spontaneous frivolity.

Still on duty today in rural areas as man's mouser, most urban cats have become indoor pets to protect them from the vagaries of a dangerous world. Many cat adoption facilities insist on this restriction for the cats for which they find homes. For, along with the cats' resurgence in popularity in recent centuries, a number of new problems have arisen to threaten the healthy existence of cats. Mother Nature has provided these beautiful creatures with a prodigious capacity to breed, and armies of feral cats roam the Earth. An estimated quarter of a million feral cats roam through the innards of the Colosseum in Rome. In the United States alone, it is estimated that the homeless and wild cat population stands at an estimated 60,000,000, every one of which is a living testament to a community's failure to implement effective spay and neuter programs. It is a miserable existence for any female cat caught in the continual cycle of litter production, and the life of the average wild tomcat isn't so pleasant either. Together, one breeding pair and their offspring can exponentially produce an estimated 400,000 cats over a seven-year period. The average lifespan of a feral cat is a mere three years, testimony to the difficulty of life without human succor.

A true "no kill" cat adoption facility will do anything and everything it can to save a cat's life and find it a safe and loving indoor home. This was the reason that Evan Kalik founded the Cat Adoption Team, which, sadly, has abandoned this philosophy in pursuit of a more "pragmatic" approach of turning away cats with special needs. This has forced Evan to disassociate himself from the organization to which he devoted thirteen years of his life and $6 million of his own personal fortune. Undeterred, Evan has turned his attention to creation of a cat sanctuary that will tend to the needs of cats that otherwise would be left to their own devices or euthanized.

Some cats, beyond the veterinary science of our time, are in such pain or are so far advanced into a terminal illness that the only merciful alternative is euthanasia. Once you have met and spoken with Evan Kalik, you know that a cat must be suffering needlessly before he will begin to consider that alternative.

The story of *Evan Kalik – The Man Who Wouldn't Kill Cats* – like so many human endeavors before it, is one of the realization of the dream of a single-minded individual who refused to listen to naysayers and worked day and night until his dream was realized. Evan is the centerpiece of this story, the history of a man suddenly struck with a deep sense of mission and commitment. His devotion to cats of every stripe would lead to the successful adoption of more than an estimated 30,000 cats. Fortunately, with that chapter ended, new ones are being written that will hopefully lead to the rescue of thousands of more cats through Evan's idea to create a cat sanctuary for "special needs" felines. That story, as well as a few of those inspired by Evan's example, is contained herein.

PART TWO

Cat Man Do

"Of all God's creatures, there is only one that cannot be made slave of the lash. That one is the cat. If man could be crossed with the cat it would improve the man, but it would deteriorate the cat."

MARK TWAIN

EVAN KALIK'S TRANSFORMATION FROM A U.S. MARINE WITH ANIMAL TROPHY heads hung on his walls as reminders of his days as a hunter, to a man who now escorts spiders from inside his home to the outside, is remarkable. His epiphany about the value of an individual life, whether animal or insect, is at the heart of his story.

Jewish Roots

He was born Evan Leon Kalik on July 10, 1938, into an Orthodox Jewish household, and lived his young life in Squirrel Hill, Pennsylvania, a Jewish community that remains to this day the focal point of Jewish life in the Pittsburgh area. When he was nine years old, the family moved to East Liberty, Pennsylvania, an area that has been around since the American Revolution.

His paternal grandparents came to America from Russia. It was from them that Evan feels certain his father inherited a toughness that he manifested throughout his life. His grandfather Kalik kept two families. Perhaps to avoid confusion in his own mind, the senior Kalik named some of the children he sire the same in both families. "If you called everybody Ben or Lewis, you were going to be right at least half of the time!" says Evan.

Evan's adopted brother, Phil, came into the household when Evan was fifteen. Leaving the house to join the U.S. Marine Corps a week before his nineteenth birthday, Evan never got to know his younger brother.

Growing up, Evan attended Hebrew school four days a week, shul on Shabbat, and Sunday school, too. In 1951, at the designated age of thirteen, Evan was Bar Mitzvahed, then at age sixteen confirmed at Sunday school, a graduation ceremony for Jewish students age sixteen to eighteen, completing their Jewish education. Ben Kalik, Evan's father, was president of an Orthodox shul, and the family attended High Holiday observances and other important dates on the Jewish calendar. Evan has observed the Yom Kippur fasting requirements since he was twelve. If one is the firstborn son in a family, the first day of Passover is also a day of fasting, and Evan honors that religious custom, as well. All of his family, as well as guests, are invited to the Kalik home for Passover Seder, a tradition in their household for decades.

Evan's mother's name was Frances. Her father, Carol, emigrated from Romania and married a Romanian girl in the U.S. She passed away at an early age in 1925, leaving behind her husband, five-year-old Frances, and Frances' older sister, Minnie. Perhaps it was that early loss that made Frances so approachable. She never hesitated to extend affection to her growing son, while Ben was more reserved with his emotional expressions. Family seemed like everything that truly mattered during Evan's boyhood, a trend away from which he is concerned. "It was so important as I grew up, but seems less and less so today. I wish that would turn around and people would rediscover how important family connections are to them."

Early Inclinations

As a youngster, Evan lived a few minutes walk from the local zoo. "A boyhood friend, Hervey Friss, and I used to visit the zoo and make plans for that day in the future when we would start our own zoo. I think I've managed as a adult to take the dream to a higher level." Evan probably inherited his love of non-human animals from his mother, who was a staunch supporter and member of the American Anti-Vivisection Society, a group founded in 1883 and, as such, the oldest non-profit animal advocacy and educational organization in the United States. Interestingly, all of Evan's pets growing up were dogs, not cats. That love affair would flourish in the distant future.

To Dream. Aye, There's the Rub

Evan recalls vivid nightmares about the Holocaust when he was a little boy, the probable result of overhearing his parents discuss the horrors of that collective blight on the human soul. It may have been then that the seed of a reverence for life was first planted within him, a seed that would lay dormant for decades before bursting open into the blossom that was to become the Cat Adoption Team in Sherwood, Oregon. The Holocaust dreams were disturbing enough to rouse him from sleep. He would venture into his parent's second-story bedroom and look out the window, looking for the Nazis he was certain were coming for him. Sometimes, after returning to his bed and falling asleep, he dreamt of shooting Nazis with a rifle.

Daydreams

Evan graduated high school in 1956. He was accepted at the University of Pittsburgh and attended classes there for one year, intending to major in business administration. He presumed he would join his father's business after graduation. He cut one class at the end of that first year, in May, intending to visit the local Marine recruitment station to ask questions about enlisting. He liked what he heard and enlisted on the spot.

Evan's earliest dreams were to be a Marine, a lumberjack, or a commercial fisherman. So he achieved one of those dreams when he enlisted in the U.S. Marine Corps in July 1957. His hero had long been General Douglas MacArthur. Like most young men with a head full of fancied heroics, Evan had no inkling of the terrors of combat, and because he joined up between the Korean "police action" and the startup of the Vietnam War, he would never be subjected to those terrors.

Semper Fi

His troop train left Pittsburgh July 4, 1957, with sixty-four other enlistees who dubbed themselves the Pittsburgh Patriots. Evan recalls the day of departure from the train station. "My high school sweetheart, who would soon become my wife, Sandra Greenberg, was with us. I had met her at a swimming pool when she was sixteen, and fell in love right then and there. My parents and grandfather were also in the car, driving through downtown

Pittsburgh. When we were about a block from the station, I bolted from the car, yelling, 'Goodbye! Love you! I'll see you!' over my shoulder. It was just so hard for me to part with the people that I cared for so much."

The train disembarked for its first stop in Washington, DC. "I felt as though I had been transported back to 1865," recalls Evan. "I remember looking out the train widow and seeing a black man with a long white beard sitting on a bale of cotton. When I got off the train, I was startled to see 'Blacks Only' and 'Whites Only' drinking fountains and restrooms. I had never seen anything like that while growing up."

A Whiff of Anti-Semitism

The train continued south to South Carolina. The men transferred to a bus that took them to the Marine Corps Recruit Depot at Parris Island. "Our sixty-five guys, and about another three-hundred or so young men, were crammed into one large room," Evan remembers. A burly sergeant told them they were to answer when their names were called, giving their Social Security number and their religion. "When I said 'Jewish,' I saw several hundred pairs of eyes look over at me. Most of them had apparently never seen a Jew before." Evan had experienced his share of anti-Semitism in Pittsburgh, but this was something new and strange.

Each recruit was given a new set of fatigues and a small cloth bag for their valuables. After a shower and very close haircut, the recruits retrieved their belongings, which they were to mail home. "When I got my felt bag back," Evan says, "I noticed that my watch was missing. I told the drill instructor that my watch was gone and he growled back, 'What do you want me to do about it?'"

Dead Eye

Evan became a crack marksman, graduating as the second best shot in his platoon after four months of basic training. He never had to perform KP duty because of his status as a member of a special rifle platoon. He was also granted the unusual privilege of making phone calls home, and on one such occasion used the privilege to propose to his high school sweetheart, Sandy.

He received a permanent personnel assignment to Parris Island after return-ing from his marriage, and was assigned to the PX.

"I was standing behind the counter one day in the PX," says Evan, "when along comes my old drill instructor. He's looking down into the glass cabinet, resting his arm on top, and I notice his watch. Sure enough, it was mine, the one that had mysteriously disappeared when I was taking a shower that first day on the base."

Watch This

Evan relayed his story to the Provost Marshall. "Can you prove it's yours?" the officer asked him. "No, I guess I can't," Evan replied. But he started think-ing about it, and decided to write to the manufacturer of the watch, after securing the serial number from the PX watch repairman, who happened to also be Jewish. The drill sergeant had left the watch to be repaired, not real-izing that he was sealing his fate by so doing. The manufacturer, the Bulova Company, confirmed that the serial number matched an order to the store in Pennsylvania where Evan had bought the watch.

Evan got his watch back, and the sergeant, a Korean War veteran, was removed from active duty responsibilities for a week. Then began a pattern of the sergeant following Evan to work everyday in his vehicle. When he had had enough, Evan stopped one day, and the man pulled up behind him. "What do you want?" Evan asked. "Why weren't you man enough to tell me about the watch?" inquired the sergeant. "I did tell you about the watch," said Evan. "Remember? You asked me, 'What do you want ME to do about it?' that first day, when I reported it missing." The sergeant abruptly turned, got back in his car, and drove away. Evan never saw the man again.

A Party of One

One morning during boot camp, a fellow trainee sidled up to Evan and asked, "See that guy over there? You better watch out for him. He's planning a 'blanket party' for you." Well known to every soldier, a "blanket party" is anything but fun for the "guest of honor." A blanket is thrown over the man, and everyone involved proceeds to give him a thorough pummel-ing. Evan thanked his informant, and the very next day, the party planner was struck by lightning while marching on the parade grounds. Once again, Evan became convinced that Providence was there to watch his back. "God wanted me around for some reason," says Evan. "I wouldn't discover that reason until many years later."

Sour Dough

When Evan was getting short – near his date of discharge from military service – a baker in Beaufort, South Carolina, about ten miles from the base, employed a man who Evan noticed was prone to anti-Semitic comments that he uttered under his breath every time the bakery delivered goods to the base. Evan discussed the matter with his commanding officer, admitting to him that the slurs were beginning to bother him. "In fact," Evan told his Captain, "if he does it again, I'm going to deck him the next time he comes in." The Captain's response was to call the baker. "If your man doesn't stop harassing my corporal about his religion, we're going to stop doing business with you." That was all it took, especially since the baker was himself Jewish. From that moment on, the baker's assistant was deferential and courteous to Corporal Evan Kalik, U.S. Marine Corps.

Married Life

Evan married Sandy on November 9, 1957, after his basic training was completed. He had to find living quarters for his new bride and himself. He rented half of a duplex. The first feedback he got on his marriage was from a staff sergeant to whom he reported for duty, who said, "If the Marine Corps had wanted you to have a wife, they would have issued you one!" One morning, when he overslept and missed roll call, the same sergeant said, "You can forget about going home. You're going to be staying on base." Once his temper cooled, the sergeant reneged, and Evan bought two alarm clocks, one within reach next to his bed, and one he located about ten feet away. He was never late for roll call again. In fact, that incident was the beginning of a lifelong habit of not just being on time, but being early for appointments.

Watering Hole

Toward the end of his tour of enlistment, Evan was reassigned from the PX to one of the base watering holes. This was somewhat ironic, for Evan did not drink alcohol. He finished his two-year tour in the Marines serving beer to his fellow jarheads, and was discharged as a Corporal.

The family decided to celebrate Evan's homecoming at the Greater Pittsburgh Airport, since one of the musicians playing in the nightclub there had played at Evan's Bar Mitzvah. Evan decided to try drinking and proceeded to consume copious amounts of alcohol, drinking an entire bottle of Canadian Club during the course of the evening. He ended up eating food from every plate at the table, then spent his twenty-first birthday in the hospital on an IV. Evan hasn't had a drink of alcohol since.

Predator

Having achieved success as a marksman while in the service, Evan took his skills into the woods and became an avid hunter. Even though he today still displays the trophies from his kills, he says he is not proud of that period of his life. "I ask God for forgiveness everyday for killing those animals, even though I never did it for pure sport, and always ate the meat from the animals I hunted. I don't kill anything anymore. I even carry insects out of my house when I find them."

Working Man

After Evan's discharge in 1959, he and Sandy lived for six months with his mother-in-law. He bought his first home while working for his father. Ben was in the scrap metal business, which he had begun in 1943. Staring out as a car wreck recycler, his dad expanded to taking electric starters and motors, removing the valuable copper from them.

Kalik and Son...Someday

Evan performed a wide range of tasks for his dad. Truck driver, crane operator, payroll preparer, swinging a hammer when the occasion called for it. Evan was, as he describes himself, "an all around schlepper!" He worked for his father for twelve and a half years. Married at age nineteen, he fathered three sons. Every time one of those sons was born his dad would say, "I'm going to make you a junior partner in the business." And every time, the promise was somehow forgotten. Evan never addressed the matter until his third son, Allan, was born. "You know," he told his father, "I'm going to take you up on your deal." His dad replied, "Okay, you get an attorney and an accountant to draw up the papers, and when they're ready, I'll sign." Evan made all the necessary arrangements, and the papers were ready in a couple of weeks. "All you have to do," Evan told his father, "is come down to the attorney's office and you and Mom can sign the papers." At the last moment, with pen in hand, his father said, "I can't do it!" "Why not?" asked Evan. "My accountant tells me if I sign, I'll only have $800 a year to live on," his father said. And that, as the saying goes, was that.

Consenting Adults

The day after the non-signing, Evan was operating a crane on the lot of his father's business when he noticed a hand reaching up to him. It was his dad, and Evan pulled him up into the cab. Ben turned to his son and said, "I hope there's no hard feelings." To which Evan replied, "No, there's no hard feelings, but I'm giving you my notice." That ended the father-son association together in business, although when his father's business finally failed years later, Evan took on the responsibility of paying off all his father's debts, for he believes in the literal interpretation of the commandment, *Honor your father and your mother, that your days may be long in the land that the Lord your God is giving you.* "It's my belief," says Evan, "that the Good Lord allowed me to eventually become a success in business so that I could fully comply with all that God expects, eventually leading me to my love and compassion for cats and every species of God's creatures. The Talmud tells me to show 'steadfast love to thousands of those who love me.' To me, that includes every creature in God's creation."

Self-Employed

A year earlier, Evan had purchased a small scrap yard, about the size of a two-car garage, from an elderly Jewish man in the neighborhood who wanted to retire. With the consummation of his career working for his father, Evan set up his own business, in effect, competing with his dad. He went to the same customers to buy the same materials he had always bought on behalf of his father, but now he was doing it for himself. No one turned him away. Evan had one paid employee that first year who sometimes showed up for work and sometimes didn't.

After going to work for himself, Evan worked so hard that he wore out some of his joints. "My wife had to pour catsup for me. I couldn't even bend my elbows from swinging a hammer all day," he said. He often received advice from friends about the wisdom of returning to work for his father, which he would have considered if his dad would live up to his word and make him part owner of the business. His mother called one day and asked if he would come back, and Evan replied, "If he keeps his word." A few days later, she called back to confirm that Ben would finally honor his promise.

Southern Horizons

His wife's two brothers had recently begun Florida Orthopedics, and Evan had given them about $1,500 to get started. He packed up the family intending to visit his brothers-in-law in Florida for two weeks, then return to Pennsylvania. Instead of spending money to fly his family to Florida, Evan decided to buy a car and make the drive south. A couple of days before the family was scheduled to get on the road, Evan's mother called to say that, once again, his father had changed his mind. The two-week visit to the Sunshine State was miserable. Evan could not tell what the future held. He knew he couldn't go back to work for his father under the old arrangement, and he knew he couldn't physically carry on by himself. The Kaliks returned home to Pennsylvania unsure of what the future held.

New Prospects

A year earlier Evan had looked at a property located about 35 miles from his house, owned by an elderly Jewish couple. He remembers that Mrs. Mildred Platt had a certain aura of class about her. "She came to the scrap yard dressed in high heeled shoes and a long fur coat." The property, located in Latrobe, Pennsylvania (Arnold Palmer's home town, and where the Pittsburgh Steelers once conducted their summer camp), consisted of a house and large garage and some acreage on which the scrap yard was located that also contained a great deal of copper. Evan bought it all for $30,000 and got most of his money back quickly by selling the copper.

Surrogate Son

One day after opening the yard for him, Mrs. Platt said to Evan, "I have some longstanding customers. Let me buy the copper with my money, and when you sell it, you pay me my money back." A bit leery and suspicious, in view of what he'd just been through with his dad, Evan reluctantly agreed. She honored that arrangement several times, and Evan made a handsome profit. He came to learn that, in her mind, Mrs. Platt had adopted Evan. She had had two sons who both died at the age of fifteen. Her daughter, Sue Platt, shared this story with Evan, saying, "You are my mother's surrogate son." Evan stayed there until 1979, making it a total of twenty years that he had been in the scrap business.

A Profound Loss

The year before, in 1978, Evan's beloved wife, Sandra, was diagnosed with breast cancer. Evan decided to sell his business and move to Florida in order to keep the extended family as close together as possible. After examining Sandy, a Florida oncologist told Evan to bring her home and enjoy together the time she still had before the cancer ended her life. "I remember going home," says Evan, "and standing in the living room of our home with my wife and three sons. Our arms wrapped around each other, we wept."

Unwilling to give up, Evan found another oncologist. Through administration of an aggressive treatment of chemotherapy and surgery, Sandra lived another five years, passing from this life on December 19, 1984, the first night of Hanukkah. "That night," says Evan, "it seemed like the walls of my home were falling down around me." He had stayed with Sandra night and day the last two weeks of her life in the hospital. He did go home the night of her death, the pain from a severe ulcer attack overwhelming him. In the middle of the night, they called him back to the hospital, and she died just moments before his arrival.

Career #2

Evan went into business as an equal partner with his brothers-in-law in Florida. "It was a real change after twenty years in the scrap business," recalls Evan. "For one thing, I can't think of many occasions in that business, except for Mrs. Platt, when I encountered women." His new business involved the manufacture of orthopedic devices. The contraption that made the business bloom was a belt designed to brace a man's back while lifting loads. Evan's oldest brother-in-law had seen the device used in a local grocery store, and brought the patent-less idea in-house. It was the mass manufacturing and marketing of these belt-braces that was to turn each of the partners into millionaires. Soon, Florida Orthopedics employed 350 workers, many of whom were women, to sew the braces and ready them for shipment all around the country. After maximizing their floor space at their plant in Opa-Locka, Florida, the partners opened a branch of the company in Dallas, Texas.

New Love

One of the many women who worked in the plant was Ardyth – Ardie, for short – who was to become Evan's new wife. "Many men are fortunate enough to be blessed once with a wonderful woman," says Evan. "I was blessed twice over." Ardie and Evan were married in 1986, the ceremony being performed at their home by Evan's ex-corporate attorney, Fred Lichstein. Prior to the formalities, Fred asked Evan, "Do you have the papers?" "Papers. What papers?" Evan inquired. He had forgotten to get a marriage license. They went ahead with the ceremony, and Evan got the "paperwork" taken care of after the honeymoon.

The Cat Jumps Over the Honeymoon

When Ardie moved into their new home with Evan, who had always considered himself a dog person, she made a request to her new husband. "I've got this old cat," she said. "Is it okay if I bring her with me?" "Sure," he replied. The "old cat," Jessie, had an eye problem. Evan found himself taking her thirty-five miles into south Miami once a week for treatments. Her eyes had been damaged by the chemicals in a lawn spray that Jessie had somehow gotten into. "I wanted a specialist to take care of my baby," is Evan's justification for that weekly round trip of seventy miles. It might have been on that stretch of highway in Florida that a new Evan emerged. "I found myself becoming increasingly concerned about not just Jessie," he says, "but cats everywhere. I began to see them on the streets wherever I went, and it really bothered me to think that they didn't have homes. I guess I started to become obsessed."

Metamorphosis

There was a change in the wind. Here was Evan Kalik, former Marine, game hunter and dog fancier, doing everything possible to help an old cat with her ailment. "I can't think of any other reason than I took the cat's need to heart," according to Evan. "She was sick, and if there was something I could do to help, by God, I was going to do it! It's the same flame that boils me to this day. If a cat is injured or ill, I can't rest until I know that it has received the best of every possible kind of available care, no matter the cost."

When Jessie died, Evan was thunderstruck. "It tore my heart out," he remembers when he thinks of that day. "Love isn't free, and when you love another, their loss is a price you have to be willing to pay. Is it worth it? William Shakespeare was so correct when he wrote 'Better to have loved and lost than never to have loved at all.'"

Evan went to a local veterinarian, Dr. Neil Tenzer, whose clinic was three minutes from Evan's house, and said, "I'll make a deal with you. I and a friend of mine will bring in any stray cat or dog we see. No matter their condition, you treat them, I'll pay for it, and you adopt them out of your hospital at no charge." That arrangement held fast for about a year, during which time Evan estimates they rescued about 150 animals at considerable cost to Evan's pocketbook. "I spent somewhere between $100,000 and $150,000 on those critters," he recalls.

Giving Back

"I am a fortunate man," says Evan. "The good Lord has watched over me for decades. I made a lot of money in Florida. It was rewarding, there's no doubt about that. But I can honestly say nothing feels as good as when I save an animal. Whether it's getting him out of harm's way or – and this is my hot button – if he or she is sick and I can get them nursed back to health. That becomes my reward. I think I'm really selfish, because I look for that feeling again and again, and receive it every single time I help a sick or wounded animal, especially cats."

Success

Evan and his family lived in Miami Beach, a few minutes' drive from

Opa-Locka. He served as the company's treasurer and salesman. He'd go directly to hospitals to sell the various products. "That business gave me the resources to make the Cat Adoption Team what it is today," says Evan. The partners sold the company in 1993 to a French bank, and Evan retired for a year after that.

Northwest Passage

After that first year's arrangement with Dr. Tenzer, the Kaliks moved to the Pacific Northwest. The business was sold in 1993, and Evan considered himself retired for the next year. Ardie's sister, Dean Black, and her husband, Loren, live in Grants Pass, Oregon, and Evan and Ardie came up occasionally to visit Dean, participating in some region-specific activities such as panning for gold. Evan was also able to indulge in one of his hobbies, collecting minerals. "I used to make spheres out of the rocks I'd find," says Evan. Through the years, he had collected a large number of rocks during his visits to Oregon, shipping them back to Florida. With the move of the Kaliks to Oregon, the rocks were headed back to their original location. "I love to work with my hands. I work with wood as well as stone. But my work with animals is what truly animates me, lights me up completely," Evan says.

The permanent move to the Pacific Northwest took place in 1994. It had taken him and Ardie seven years to find the perfect house, which they finally settled on in Sherwood, Oregon. "We fell in love with the place immediately," he says, and it's easy to understand why. Their 4,300 square foot home sits on twenty-five acres of land that produces apples, plums, grapes, hazelnuts, walnuts, cherries, two varieties of pears, and a vegetable garden.

Kalik-land

A barn on the property was built in 1931 and is registered as an historic building. It sits to the back of the house, and Evan has built three additional barns since taking up residence. In keeping with his love of animals, he has three llamas, three horses, and two angora goats, in addition to the twelve house cats (two of them are three-legged) who seem to inhabit every corner of their home. "I built an atrium off the side of the house to let those cats that wish it to have a bit of outdoors fresh air. But just like the cats that I have put up for adoption," Evan says, "all my babies are indoors, away from the coyotes and all the other dangers that come with living outside."

Planting New Roots

Finding and taking care of stray animals wasn't on Evan's radar when he first moved to Oregon. There were so many distractions presented in getting settled, not the least of which was getting two of his sons, Allan and Eric, who had moved to the Northwest with him, settled into a business. His oldest son, Eric, had been the top salesman with Florida Orthopedics. After searching for opportunities, father and sons decided to buy Anchor Fireplace Products in Northwest Portland. The boys stayed in business at that location for four years, until 1998. "We thought the business was doing well," says Evan. "I stayed away from the books and selling, lending a hand where I could when any physical labor was required, like loading a truck."

A C.A.T. is Born

In 1998, his sons decided to move the enterprise closer to where they lived in Sherwood. "I made a deal with my sons," Evan says. "I would build them a 25,000-square-foot building for their business if they would give me 3,000 square feet on the second floor that they would otherwise have used for storage. I wanted to have a cat shelter that wasn't burdened by a monthly rent or mortgage payment," Evan says.

Thus were the beginnings of C.A.T., the Cat Adoption Team of Sherwood, Oregon. The doors opened on May 1, 1998. "I told Ardie I was going to start with ten cats," says Evan. When the architect who had designed and built the building had given Evan the drawings for his 3,000 square feet upstairs, he had envisioned thirty cages behind glass. Evan realized that with the addition of another eighteen inches of glass to the top of the cages, he could put two rows of cages in without costing him that much extra money. And so, there were sixty cages when the grand opening ribbon was cut, cages that Evan filled in the first week of the shelter. "That spoke directly to the tremendous need," according to Evan.

Spreading the Word

"The word must have gotten out that some old screwball was spending money on stray cats like a drunken sailor in port," Evan says. He had been utilizing the services of some local veterinarians, and a local cat enthusiast, Heather Heinz, also came to Evan with strays. The existence of C.A.T. became known virtually overnight throughout the Portland metropolitan area. "In the beginning, I answered the phones at the shelter," Evan concedes, "but I had to stop doing that because I didn't know how to say 'no,' and there was only so much room at C.A.T."

Three Musketeers + Ten

Evan, Ardie, one paid employee, and ten volunteers constituted the newly formed C.A.T., at that time a private 501(c)3 non-profit organization set up by Evan. "We had no medical staff," says Evan, "so any care the cats needed, I had to pay for out of my pocket to an outside veterinarian." He, Ardie, and their one staff member used to do all the cage and litter box cleaning and cat feeding, as well as administering any medications the various cats required. "We would finish the morning rounds and it would be time to start the evening rounds. Ardie and I were usually there until ten or eleven each evening. They were very long days, one right after another."

The Cost of Compassion

As the shelter grew, veterinarians sometimes came to C.A.T. to administer their care. At the same time, it was still common for Evan to cart a cat off to some vet's office many times a week. He was spending between $8,000 and $9,000 per month on his little four-legged wards and began to realize the wisdom – the necessity – of having an on-site veterinary hospital. "I'd call around to local vets and tell them I had twenty-five cats that needed spaying today," Evan remembers. "They'd tell me, 'Great, bring in one today, and two tomorrow,' and so on. I knew I couldn't get the job done expecting outside clinics to do all the work."

Stop-Gap Measure

There was a very short period of time during which Evan allowed cats to be adopted out of the clinic without being spayed or neutered. He would charge a $40 premium that was refundable once he was presented with proof that the animal had been fixed. "My bottom line was to get the cats a home, so I could continue to take in new cats, find them homes, and so on down the line." In the beginning also, Evan had the cats declawed. "I didn't know any better," he says in his own defense. "Now that I realize how painful that procedure is – it would be like a human having each of their fingers cut off at the last joint – I would never do that to a cat again."

A C.A.T. Cat Forever

Evan also established the policy wherein any cat that passes through the doors of C.A.T. would have a permanent sanctuary. The way he saw it, "C.A.T. was a little piece of heaven – a haven – that should always belong to our cats as long as each of them is alive." During Evan's association with C.A.T., if an adopter brought a cat back one year or ten years after adopting it, that cat was welcomed back to C.A.T. until another home could be found. "If I didn't do that," says Evan, "the cat is either going to be dumped by the side of the road or put into a shelter when it will be euthanized after thirty days or so." Unfortunately, when C.A.T. became a public non-profit organization, Evan lost control of the organization's policies and, in 2011, he reluctantly resigned from the board of directors when it became evident that the "forever cat" policy was apparently being dropped.

Indoors Only, Please

Another of Evan's ideas – that every adopter agree to keep their cats indoors – was also adopted by the organization he founded. "It's too dangerous for a domestic cat to live out-of-doors anymore," Evan says. He has seen first hand what sometimes happens to cats when they live outside, from becoming the victims of predators or careless drivers, to those disturbed individuals who will find an animal to torture. Evan was adamant about this policy. "I started to fall in love with each and every cat that came to us, and I still feel that way. Their middle names are all Kalik, and I will care about their welfare, each and every one of them, until the day they die. Or I die, whichever comes first."

Refurbishment

Evan wanted the expertise of someone in the field before building an onsite hospital, so he called a veterinarian he knew and with his consultation, Evan spent $156,000 building a 1,950 square foot facility downstairs and another 1,950 square feet upstairs at C.A.T. As his sons' business began to fail, Evan took over their showroom space downstairs. Upstairs, they extended the building outwards to accommodate the new hospital. Evan hired Dr. Kris Ottoman to head the medical department. "What was best for the animals was my concern throughout the building process," says Evan. "Whatever they needed, I was willing to pay for."

Evan's Hot Buttons

For Evan, the hospital was a central point for his efforts to save cats and kittens. He derives most of his joy from bringing a sick or injured cat back to wellness. Getting them a good adoptive home runs a close second. "I used to want to go to the home of the adopting family to see if the environment was good enough for one of my cats," he says. "Of course, that isn't possible. I had to resist the urge to go banging on doors to make certain my cats were thriving." Evan's cell phone still rings with calls from like-minded people who know that he won't say no when it comes to saving animals. "Cats are still my primary love, but I have helped place horses, pot-bellied pigs and goats, as well as a cow named Ms. Heidi. If an animal needs a home, I'm on the case."

PART THREE

Evan's Ark

"I am in favor of animal rights as well as human rights. That is the way of a whole human being."

ABRAHAM LINCOLN

Knee Deep

The first horse Evan acquired came as a result of his search for a trailer. He had located a trailer for sale and while taking a look at it, he noticed a horse standing behind a fence in water up to his knees. He walked over and began talking to the horse and the owner waltzed over and said, "Hey, he likes you!" Evan thought, "Sure he likes me. He'd like anybody who could distract him from the discomfort of standing in knee-deep water." The rest of the story is classic Evan Kalik. He bought the trailer *and* the horse.

Blue on Blue

Dandy the work horse became an immediate learning experience, Evan never having owned a horse before. He had only had Dandy a couple of months when one of the lessons turned quite harsh. While trying to get Dandy into a stable one day, he kicked Evan squarely in the head with his hind legs, catching him under the left eye. He ended up flat on his back but his reflexes brought him straight back up again. His vision seemed altered and he wondered if his first equine adventure was going to lead to permanent eye damage. Closer examination of his glasses revealed that Dandy's well-placed punt had knocked the lens out of the left side of the glasses. "The cut under my eye took eight stitches to close during a visit to the hospital, but it was the last time I stood behind a horse," says Evan. "They can really use those hind feet as a weapon when they're scared or angry. My black-and-blue and swollen closed eye raised a few eyebrows for a time after that, and of course, everyone asked what the other guy looked like. I had to confess that Dandy came out ahead, not that I would have for a moment considered taking revenge on him. He was doing what came natural to him, and that is something I wish more people would take into consideration when they are dealing with animals. Our fellow creatures have reactions and instincts that they exhibit without fail under certain conditions, and it's up to us to learn how to work our way around those realities without expecting the animal to act with the same rational restraint available to humans. Of course, people often react when driven by their compulsions, so perhaps we're not as different from non-human animals as we would like to think we are."

One Plus Two

Two other horses came along to provide company for Dandy. Evan adopted a pregnant female, Miss Meri, who soon provided a foal he named Ripcord. In the last few years, two of them have become highly allergic to hay, and this creates a great deal more work for Ardie and Evan, as during the allergy season – the spring and summer – they require frequent inhalation therapy when they have difficulty breathing. Evan always has a wry smile when describing the treatments. "You haven't lived until you've tried to give a horse such a treatment, which involves putting a mask around their nose while trying to keep the horse calm and focused. They tend to flip their heads up in an attempt to avoid the mask, and you go flying with them." The horses also need injections, one getting a weekly needle, the other receiving a twice-monthly inoculation. Once a year, there is the tooth filing ritual because a horse's teeth continue to grow.

Three-card Monte

Another situation involving equines began when Evan received a phone call from a women looking for help with a sick cat. She had no money and said she didn't know where else to turn. She promised to pay him back but he never received back any portion of the $3,500 he spent on the cat. "So be it," he says. "It was good for the animal and great for me to be able to save its life." Not long thereafter, the same woman called again with a tale about a horse and her colts and foals that needed rescuing, saying Evan could step in and save them for $650. She went on to claim that if he didn't act soon, a meat packing company from France was coming soon to turn the horses into food! She claimed further that another horse awaiting a similar fate could be saved for $450. As he had done and would do again on many such occasions, Evan called his friend Carol Laughlin, knowing she cares as much for animals as does he. She, in turn, recommended Chris Miles, a fellow animal lover who she thought could accommodate the horses. Upon arrival at the location where the horses were supposedly available, Chris was told those horses had been sold, but there were others who needed rescuing. Chris smelled a rat, not a horse. "Since this occurrence, I have learned that this is a common scam pulled frequently by unscrupulous individuals who identify animal lovers with monetary resources as their marks," says Evan.

Starving Equines

Soon after this not-so-elevating affair, Chris was online one day and read about a veterinarian who had rescued thirty horses found by the authorities. The animals were starving on a piece of rural property. One of the horses had worn its teeth to nubs by trying to survive eating tree bark. The local veterinarian in the story took all the thirty horses, treated them for their varying ailments, bringing them back to a state of health. She was given permission to recoup her expenses by selling the horses. Chris called Evan, and he had her husband stop by and he gave him $800 in cash to buy at least one of the horses. She adopted an animal named Mandy (same name as one of Evan's cats) for $150, and he told her to use some of the rest of the money to buy feed and get the horse's hoofs tended to, which cost $450. Shortly thereafter, Chris's husband, a man Evan had never met before giving him the cash, returned $200, the balance of the money left over. "There are kind, decent, honest people in the world," says Evan. "You just don't know when you first associate with someone whether or not they will turn out to be one of them. In order to save an animal's life, I'm still willing to take the chance."

Dolly Llamas

When Ardie and Evan bought their home and property in Sherwood, Oregon, the deal came with two llamas. Neither of these two South American critters ever got along. "I guess animals have as difficult a time cooperating with one another as people sometimes do," muses Evan. Eventually acquiring a female Evan named Kareem, he enjoyed assisting her as she gave birth to another female that was born with a deformed nose, one that embarks its way off her face at an almost 45-degree angle. "Many think llamas aren't the most attractive animals to begin with, but my little Consuela has had a particular challenge in presenting an attractive façade to the world. I love her no less for it!" It is an emotional blow whenever one of our animal companions departs the Earth, and Evan eventually lost Kareem. One morning he found her near death, and sat in a field, softly cradling her head until she passed away. "We have an unwritten, unspoken agreement with those we love," says Evan. "We know that, at some point, either they will die or we will. Yet who would sacrifice the love we get and give one another during life, just to avoid the pain of separation. That said, I loved that old llama, and will always miss her."

It's Enough to Get Your Goat

Evan received a call one day from a woman who told him of eight angora goats, thirty-nine chickens, and a few other birds who were being rescued from an abusive owner. He was able to make one phone call that took care of getting all of the birds a place to live and thrive, and he decided to keep two of the angora goats. "These animals are among the sweetest I care for," claims Evan. "One, Eli, insists on being the alpha male with the other, Herman, and bullies him quite a bit, but the two have become part of the Kalik menagerie here at our Sherwood, Oregon, property." With people, Eli is a lover not a fighter, enjoying having his ears and chin rubbed and getting his back patted. Herman is standoffish but seems to enjoy eating and whatever else it is that delights a goat. Both of them practically inhale the grain Evan and Ardie give them every day. "I guess that's being as hungry as a goat!" laughs Evan. Because they grow about half an inch of mohair a month, they must be sheared twice a year, which means that someone, someday,

Photos

Evan gets his back scratched the
surefire way from an Ocelot during
a visit to Oregon Wildcat Haven.

"What's that behind your ear?" Whatever
a cougar asks you, you should tell him.
But Evan shows no fear during this
interaction at the C.A.T. hospital.

Susie Belle is another
of the more than
30,000 cats that
Evan took in to the
Cat Adoption Team
after he founded
that organization.

Wild-eyed beauty Rosa was adopted from a PetSmart® after getting healthy at C.A.T.

Misha and Abby are just two of the more than 30,000 cats whose lives Evan has saved.

Suzie gave birth to the first litter born at C.A.T. The kitties, as always, want their milk!

Gaucho seems completely at ease and filled with
confidence in her new home after her adoption.

Santa Evan had a cat for every kid at Christmas when he
was with the organization he founded, the Cat Adoption
Team – even if they were naughty and not nice.

Louise and Tom share a chair. Louise is Evan's "rabbi cat" who accompanies him during his evening devotionals.

Sunshine and Louise take an afternoon break from their morning nap.

Sunshine assumes a strange smile-like expression the Kaliks call "bottom face" during one of the more delicate moments of her self-grooming.

Tongue bath completed,
it's time for Sunshine
to take another nap.

Riley, one of the Kalik's
three-legged kitties,
is always ready to
offer his services as
official greeter when
visitors come to the
Kalik residence.

Riley and Tomcat,
the other three-
legged beauty in the
Kalik household.

Tomcat gets around just fine, thank you, with just three legs.

Lulu believes that Evan's shoulders and head provide the best view in the house.

Banjo spends all his time in Ardie and Evan's bedroom. He always wins the staring contests.

Mandy keeps a sharp eye on the activity at the bird feeder.

Arthritic Pepper needs a baby aspirin three times a week, as well twice monthly injections, to ward off her symptoms.

Chester, the cat who once reached out his paw to comfort Evan at a critical moment, manages to navigate life with one eye and a huge heart.

Rossi, a diabetic cat who sat in a cage for over a year because no one wanted to take on the responsibilities of such a high-maintenance animal. The Kaliks give him insulin injections twice a day. And she knows how to ask Ardie for affection.

Elvira receives her meds from Evan. It is all part of the ongoing routine at the Kalik household.

Timpani likes to hang out with Evan every morning, especially because Evan places droplets of water on the tub's edge for her to drink.

Ghostbuster reminds us that no matter how "domesticated" a cat may become, they are still a part of the wild.

"Yeah, what do you want?" seems to be the question for Emma cat as she tries to nap after being adopted.

A friendship and cat conspiracy has grown between Ardie, Evan, and David.

Bishop the Praying Cat could be offering up thanks that Evan is around to take care of needy kitties like him.

There is nothing quite as mysterious and soothing as the eyes of a cat. Just ask Evan.

Evan petting kitty.

Evan is not one to euthanize a cat because it has FIV, the cat version of HIV. He has saved the lives of many cats with FIV, like Paul. These cats can enjoy life as much as any of God's creatures. One way Paul enjoyed himself was to sit on Evan's shoulders for the view.

These three kittens apparently do not mind a communal bowl of milk while they await a Forever Home and their newly chosen names.

Like so many felines, Aja owes her life to Evan and expresses
her gratitude by doing what cats do – dozing off.

It's difficult to believe that these photos depict the same dog, before and after
"Evan care." Evan rescued him in Florida before he and Ardie moved to Oregon.
He had lost all his hair and was almost unapproachable suffered, as well as the
wounds he received after being struck by a car, including a compound fracture of
the tail! Lots of rehabilitation and TLC later, Evan put the pooch up for adoption.

Even when his cats pass away, Evan keeps a special place for each one of them in his heart. Yoda is one such cat.

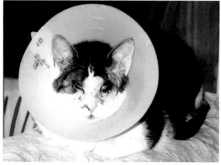

Evan found Buddy wandering around Beaverton, Oregon, with a nasty wound, the apparent result of an encounter with a raccoon. Although Buddy lost one eye, several thousand dollars' worth of surgery saved his life. He was adopted by Layne Slabe, who enjoys the company of the one-eyed lap cat named Buddy.

Evan nursed Budster back to health. When he came to
Evan, Budster had not one hair on his body.

In "Evan World" even cats and
dogs learn to get along!

At the Kalik ranch, it's always break time.

Some cats, like Cecil, have to make a roundabout journey before finding a Forever Home. She went from six months in a pet store before being adopted for eleven months, then heading to C.A.T. for another fourteen months. Finally, Cecil was adopted into a home where he has been ever since.

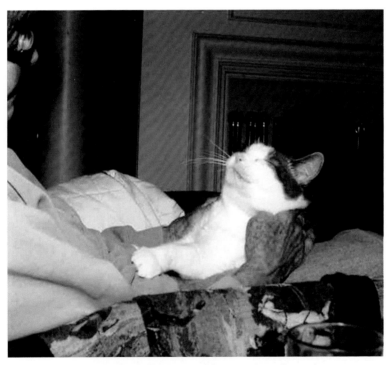

Doing what cats do best – soaking up love from their human companions – Mandy appreciates Ardie's attentions. Evan received Mandy as a present on his 73rd birthday.

Dana Gilbert has opened her heart and her home to terminally ill cats that need hospice care during their final days. A very special kind of compassion is required for this kindness.

How could anyone resist this face? Ally Cat found a home after a short stay with Evan.

Biscuit was the first feline cancer survivor to be cured at C.A.T. Evan considered every life saved a major victory. "The Talmud says if you save one life, you save the world" are words that Evan lives by.

Grace Kelly became depressed and appeared to have given up hope of ever being adopted, when the magic moment came and she found a new home.

Green Velvet had to wait eighteen months before someone gave her a Forever Home. It is a much greater challenge to find a home for an adult cat than for a kitten

The silhouette of Gus the Duck outside the Kalik's backdoor. Gus came closer than a duck would want to becoming dinner for a hawk. Fate and Evan Kalik intervened to give Gus a new lease on life.

Hannah, one of the first cats Evan rescued, was pregnant when she was hit by a car. The accident broke two of her legs and caused the litter to be lost, but Hannah fully recovered and was adopted to a Forever Home.

Evan and Ardie agree that it's the Cat's meow having twelve cats around the house.

Courtesy of Leanne Miller Photography

I'm a
**Hurricane
Katrina**
Survivor

Cindy Morrison spearheaded
efforts to save as many cats as
possible after Hurricane Katrina
hit the Gulf Coast during the 2005
Atlantic hurricane season. Through
the efforts of volunteers, fifty-one
cats were brought back to Portland
for medical care and adoption.

The fully equipped hospital at C.A.T., built entirely with Evan's funding, was a place where cats received state-of-the-art veterinary care. It is Evan's dream to create a mobile clinic that will take care of cats in the proposed Cat Alliance Team Sanctuary (CATS). Evan is hoping to solicit helping in financing the hiring of a full time veterinarian and two vet techs.

Merlot, another C.A.T. alumnus, was eventually adopted by a C.A.T. volunteer.

Sometimes even seniors can find a home. Mr. Handsome was thirteen years old when he was finally taken in by a loving family.

Many a kitten, like this little beauty, has entered the world thanks to the safety offered to their moms by Evan.

Part of the everyday feeding ritual at the Kalik house includes the goats Evan rescued. Ardie enjoys a moment with Eli, while Herman rules the barn as a loner.

All horses, goats, and llamas present and accounted for on the Kalik pasture.

Does the universe reach out to us with messages we'll never completely understand? Whatever the explanation, Evan noticed a very identifiable shadow cast in his bathroom by a randomly hung towel.

Look again. There is a black cat, too! Taco and Mae pose
as the Yin and Yang of the feline world.

A beautiful, sweet cat, Kiria died
too young of cancer. But her
short life was made better during
the time she was fostered.

Evan is building a new cat sanctuary and needs donations to make it a success.

The Cat Alliance Team Sanctuary building nears completion in mid-2013.

The new CATS sanctuary will be divided into sections, each devoted to the loving care and refuge of cats with special needs.

Evan has spared no expense in creating a cat sanctuary that will last for many years.

Nearing completion, the cat sanctuary structure will provide a
home for cats that would otherwise face euthanasia.

Pepper, one of the Kalik's twelve house cats, won't melt in your hand, but Evan
is certain that her winning ways will probably melt a little bit of your heart.

Tommy, a 3-legged cat, likes to hang out in the Kalik's bedroom most of the day.

Chester (L) and Louise (R) enjoy being as close to Evan as they can get.

Mandy, Chester and Lulu's mother, was a 73rd birthday present for Evan, who is easy to buy for. Just get him another cat!

Lulu, who enjoys sitting on Evan's head whenever the opportunity arises.

Rossie is apparently waiting for an important call.

Louise is Evan's rabbi who prays with him every night.

Elvira is another member of the Upstairs Club at the Kalik domicile.

Banjo, like any good feline, appreciates the chance to
be the center of photographic attention.

Evan and Ardie are happiest when they are surrounded by their feline friends.

Rossie reaches out to Ardie whenever he feels the need for some extra TLC.

will probably benefit from a few nice sweaters. Ardie keeps bags full of mohair but the preparation and spinning process is quite involved, so the Kaliks are still in the think-about-it stage. When the goats first arrived, Evan kept them in the barn until they felt a little more secure. When it came time to let them out into the field, they bolted through the llama pasture and under a wire fence right into the pasture where the horses stay. The horses jumped into action, chasing them in circles until they had them rounded up in the center of the field. That was too much for the goats, who proceeded to run back under the wire fence and straight back into the barn. It took several days before they were brave enough to venture out again, this time avoiding the horse pasture.

Wanna Buy a Duck?

The saying has it that life is stranger than fiction, and this is one of those stories. It all began at breakfast time one morning. Evan looked out in the backyard and there stood a duck at his back door. He went about his morning routine and, every so often, he checked to see if the duck had moved on. The duck remained in place. "By lunchtime, I finally got the message from the Good Lord," says Evan, "and decided that this avian fellow wasn't going away. I dialed up a friend, Carol Laughlin, who said she would look after his welfare." Carol, in turn, called a veterinarian in nearby Newberg, Oregon, and told them about Evan's new-found friend. He scooped up the duck and placed him in a fenced pen behind the barn, a refuge that came complete with a shelter. He put him there because the vet couldn't tend to avians until the next day. Concerned about a coyote invasion, Evan carefully checked the fence and it seemed intact. Just to make certain, he used some wire and fixed what could have been a potential coyote entrance hole on the gate. Satisfied that no critters were going to get in or out, he turned his attention to his next task.

Where, Oh, Where Has My Little Duck Gone?

Having no experience in duck diet, Evan drove to a feed store and acquired some grain. He put a bowl of grain in one bowl and water into another, placing them where the duck would have easy access in its temporary home.

The next morning, Evan's phone rang and a friend inquired about the duck's health. Putting the phone down, he walked out to check. The yard was quiet and the duck was nowhere to be found. His food had been mixed – water into the grain, grain into the water. "I guess that's how ducks like their food," Evan says, "but I couldn't find him anywhere. I could find no breaches in the fence or gate, no tunnels dug under it, no feathers or other signs of a struggle. I was totally baffled." His car was due in the garage for repairs that day, so off Ardie went in the car, Evan following in his pickup truck, still trying to understand what had happened to the duck. An alien ab-duck-tion, perhaps? Suddenly, there in the middle of the road, a duck appeared, walking in confused circles with blood flowing from the top of his head and from his ear. Once again scooping up the duck, Evan called the vet and asked if I could bring him in right away, as now he was injured.

Gus the Duck

As another first in his life as an animal rescuer, Evan learned how to use an oral pill injector on a duck, as a vet technician held him steady. From there, he took the injured bird to a friend, Carol Laughlin again, who had a perfect place for the bird's recuperation, a parcel of net-covered land with a small pond. Here, for certain, nothing could get in or out to bother Gus, which is what Evan's feathered pal soon assumed as a given name.

Bird Tale

A week later, the young woman who cleans Evan's barn came to work with a tale to tell. She recounted her strange experience of a week before, coming to work and seeing a hawk flying overhead with a duck in his talons. He had gained altitude coming up over the fence behind Evan's barn and there was nothing she could do to intervene. She completed her work, and on the way home, noticed what she thought was a dead duck in the road. This must have been minutes before Ardie and Evan came along, giving the duck enough time to revive sufficiently to wander in confused circles. Somehow, this resurrected duck had managed to squirm its way out of the hawk's talons. Mystery solved! "This is another of those cases where I see God's intervention when it comes to my role as animal rescuer," says Evan.

"If anyone chooses to dismiss this as chance, I think that the real juice in the story is being squeezed out. I cannot see this other than one of heaven's small miracles on behalf of one of its creations." Hopefully, the hawk found itself another lunch somewhere. Gus was evidently not meant to supply himself as the hawk's midday meal that day. Instead, Evan was meant to save him. "This is my joy. Instead of collecting cars, boats or houses, I like to collect saved lives. It gives great meaning to my heart and soul."

From My Mouth to God's Ears

Each night before he retires, Evan recites the names of his feline friends, giving them ultimately into the arms of God. "I do believe that while God ultimately cares for us all, He expects us to act as stewards and caregivers for animals," Evan says. "Especially those we have domesticated and made dependent upon us." He keeps a list of the cats he has rescued through the years who have died, many of whose ashes reside in a place of memorial in his office. "I pray for their tiny souls each night before bed, as well. This may be the greatest sadness of committing ourselves to a relationship with domestic animal companions. Their lifespans are much shorter than ours, and we know going into the relationship that we are likely to have to mourn their passing." Yet Evan embraces this process, believing that what he receives from them while they are alive is worth the pain of loss and separation that comes with their passing. "Besides, I'm getting up there in years," he says, "and am likely to leave some of my little friends behind. They will be well taken care of in my will, and my hope is that somehow, somewhere in another dimension that some call heaven, I will see them all again."

Current Feline Friends

There are twelve cats sharing Ardie and Evan's home today. All are rescue cats of one stripe or another, including two cats with only three legs, one diabetic cat, and one with a thyroid condition. Some have bad eyes, but every one of them is a precious sentient being that affords the Kaliks unbounded love and companionship. It is indeed a great deal of feeding and litter box emptying, not to mention substantial vet bills, but God has blessed Evan with the means to afford these necessities for them, and he gladly offers them what he has rather than spending it on himself. It is still not uncommon for him to spend $500 or more on a single cat that needs some sort of medical treatment right after its rescue. There was a time when such expenditures meant nothing to Evan, but his estate has diminished to the point where he must stop for a moment and consider the amount he is spending money on vet bills before he does so. He has never refused to help a cat that needed it but he feels the need to at least be more discerning about how he expends funds these days, which is why he is always on the lookout for like-minded animal lovers who can perhaps help with some of the costs of caring for the cats he rescues.

The twelve cats that presently share the house with Ardie and Evan (or, perhaps, who allow their humans to live there, too!) are as follows:

<u>Riley</u> – One of Evan's three-legged beauties. Riley lost his right leg after a severe dog bite. "He's a gregarious fellow, always ready to greet visitors to our home. He happens to be one of David Michael Smith's favorites, and comes out to greet David whenever he comes to our home, hopping up onto the kitchen table, as nimble as can be with just his three legs."

<u>Tomcat</u> – Another three-legged pal who was rescued by a friend of Evan's, Louis Caruso, who lives south of Salem, Oregon. A veterinarian in that area tried to save Tomcat's leg after an accident of some unknown cause, but to no avail. He's thriving now, if anything, thriving too much! Tomcat has put on a lot of weight, but he seems to enjoy living upstairs in the Kalik household, sleeping between Ardie and Evan every night.

<u>Sunshine</u> – Louis also brought this wonderful cat into Evan's life, at the same time that he gave him Tomcat. C.A.T. was not permitting Evan to bring any more cats to them, so he had his friend Lou bring Sunshine into Salem Friends of Felines. They, in turn, took him to the Salem Humane Society, from whom C.A.T. would accept cats! From there, Evan scooped him up forthwith. Sometimes the road to salvation is a convoluted one.

<u>Chester</u> – One of Evan's "bad eye" kitties who has a clouded membrane over his left eye that doesn't seem to slow him down a bit. A specialist managed to save the eye with a medication regimen. It is well documented that cats

help humans reduce their stress level. Petting a cat is known to lower blood pressure. Evan says, "I recall a recent instance when Chester played the central role in calming me down. Arthritic hands caused me to knock over two jars of homemade plum preserves and I was angry with myself. I was griping away while brushing my teeth, and up walked Chester. He gently placed a paw on my free hand, and I swear to you, I felt the anger just drain completely out of my body, from rage to serenity in an instant! Did this cat sense my mood and reach out to offer me a tranquil touch of his energy, perhaps directed to do so from some Higher Power? I have no scientific proof, but you can't convince me otherwise."

Lulu – Chester's sister is prone to sitting on Evan's head, perhaps because of the view from up there. A wonderful, loving, magical cat companion, according to Evan.

Mandy – Chester and Lulu's mom, a happy cat now that she does not have to worry about producing one litter of kitties after another. Three other kittens from the litter that included Chester and Lulu were adopted by other families. Evan tried to have Mandy adopted out but ended up asking Ardie to retrieve her for him as a birthday present. "One of the nicest gifts I have ever received," he smiles.

Rossi – A diabetic cat that sat in a cage for over a year because no one wanted to take on the responsibilities associated with such a high maintenance animal. Another Kalik friend and animal lover, Mary Hardy, picked him up at the vet's office every day and took him home for about an hour. She asked if Evan would find him a home, and he tried to no avail, so he brought him to the Kalik residence. Rossi requires subcutaneous insulin injections twice a day. "I think it is fascinating how cats are subject to many of the same maladies that humans suffer," Evan says, "and the remedies for them are remarkably similar or the same." At one time, a feline specific insulin was manufactured but there must not have been large enough a market for it because it is no longer offered. Rossi is given human insulin and seems to respond well, although it took the Kaliks a long time to discover the right dosage for him.

Elvira – She receives a pill twice every day, different doses at 7:30 AM and 7:30 PM, for a thyroid condition. A diminutive kitty, Elvira used to live rent free in the guest house on the Kalik property. She is now one of the clowder of kitties who live upstairs in the main house where Ardie and Evan reside.

Pepper – She is an arthritic kitty who needs a baby aspirin three times a week, -as well as twice-monthly injections, to ward off her symptoms. Pepper once roamed the alleyways of Ft. Lauderdale, Florida. "Thanks to the rescue efforts of my brother, she has come a long way from those environs and those days, I'm happy to report," Evan says.

Louise – On one occasion, a volunteer at C.A.T. adopted two cats and reported back that her vet claimed there was a mite infestation at C.A.T. Evan panicked and called another local vet to come in and take care of the supposed problem. It cost him $1,500 to get every cat inoculated, including Louise. "This little gal had an allergic reaction and was splayed out on the floor like a bear rug, shaking and not looking so well," remembers Evan. "I called another dedicated veterinarian I knew at the time who took Louise home for two weeks and nursed her back to health – another $1,500. Another story of life succeeding over the odds against it, even if it did take $3,000! I called the volunteer back, and she said that the original vet who had raised the initial red flag had found just one mite between the two cats. Hardly an infestation, but I would rather have spent the money than have taken any chances." Today, Louise is fine, and Evan thinks of her as his feline rabbi. Each evening she likes to sit on his desk as he says his prayers. "I'd almost swear she joins in with me."

Timpani – This was one of those instances where the cat decides to adopt the human rather than the other way around. Timpani was standing at Evan's back door one day, and when Ardie heard her meowing, she opened the door and in walked Timpani as much as to say, "Okay, thanks, I live here now!" Evan believes God puts cats and other animals in need right in his path, or leads them to his door, so he can help them. It has happened too often to brush aside as mere coincidence. Timpani now plays the role of Evan's guardian. He takes a bath every morning to prepare him for the day's onslaughts, and Timpani jumps up on the side of the tub to watch over him. "I make small puddles of water along the edge of the tub that she enjoys drinking. One day she took a record twenty-three drinks! Good thing she doesn't drive, I'd have to cut her off. At night, she likes to snuggle up into the small of my back. It doesn't get any better than this."

Banjo – This boy falls into that unfortunate category of "inappropriate peeing." Most human companions will not put up with this behavior, which Evan is convinced often has some psychological component of abuse associated with it. That is, if the problem cannot be traced to a urinary tract infection. The difficulties changing this behavior are legion, yet Evan is convinced that with patience and time, coupled with certain strategies, sometimes the behavior can be altered. Changing litter sometimes helps. Cats prefer fine-grained unscented litter and will let you know when they don't like what you're using. What also works is making sure to scoop the litter box daily, and with multiple cats, scoop twice daily. Cats often refuse to use dirty boxes. Also, do not place litter boxes right next to each other because the cat might interpret the two boxes as one and then refuse to use the second box if the first box has any old urine or feces in it. New litter boxes are also sometimes in order. If litter boxes are old, they may have absorbed odors even if they are regularly cleaned. Old urine spots on the rug or elsewhere must be thoroughly cleaned, as well. If a cat can smell the old urine, he or she will think that place is a good place to pee. Using a fluorescent black light is the best way to find old urine. Treat all old spots with an enzymatic cleanser. Or, try putting a plastic carpet runner upside down on the places they like to pee. Most cats don't like to walk on the "spikes" so they will avoid the covered spots. Another tactic, put something that has a strong odor where the cat likes to pee. Most cats hate the smell of citrus, so putting citrus-scented air freshener or orange peels or citrus potpourri where he or she pees will make them shy away. Banjo has made progress, still having some instances of inappropriate peeing that the Kaliks are willing to tolerate.

Care and Feeding

Without Ardie to help, Evan knows he could not handle all the responsibility associated with so many cats and other animals. "I thank her from the bottom of my heart for the care and love she shows each individual cat every day of our lives and theirs," he says. "Additionally, I have hired two helpers who come to us in the mornings to feed the goats, llamas, and horses and to clean their stalls seven days a week. Ardie and I take the end of the day shift." This involves corralling everyone into the barn, feeding them, and giving them any special medical treatments they might require from time to time. The Kaliks usually spend about an hour so occupied each early evening. Cats normally like two to four feedings a day, so it seems like that is going on most of the time throughout the day. Litter boxes fill their upstairs, with six in the bathroom, three in the bedroom, and a few more scattered about amongst spare bedrooms. A few more occupy various rooms downstairs. Physical incapacitation due to a bad shoulder has made it difficult for Evan to help with cleaning the boxes but, again, Ardie seems to embrace the task without complaint. "I know how much effort it requires, and I try to let her know frequently how much I appreciate her hard work."

Atrium Access

With that many cats roaming about, despite the fact that the Kaliks occupy a large home, Evan feels it is necessary to provide the animals with a little access to out-of-doors ambiance. He thus built an atrium which they can use as they feel the necessity to get a little fresh air. "I know it's not the same as being able to roam freely in the world," Evan admits, "but I think it is a step up from being predator food for coyotes and other beasties of the natural world that still roam or fly about looking for a meal."

Animal Intelligence

"Cats, like all animals," says Evan, "are a great deal smarter than we usually give them credit for. Injured or just plain homeless strays find me all the time. Sometimes they simply wander up my driveway, letting me know they need a home and the love and comfort that comes with it." It is this unusual affinity between cat and man that has prompted Evan to make plans for a cat sanctuary, the next incarnation of his role as a cat lover.

Money Isn't the Issue

Evan claims that, "If someone came to me and said, 'I'll give you $10 million and you can do with it whatever you want to save cats, but you have to take every single animal that comes your way,' I'd say, 'No, thank you.' Why? Because that would force me into euthanizing animals in order to make room for the ever expanding number that would come to us." So it is that Evan adopted another cardinal rule in his methods of treating cats. "I will never euthanize a cat, unless they have a fatal disease, are in pain that cannot be alleviated and they won't eat." During all of the time that Evan was at C.A.T., it was strictly a "no kill," or "limited intake" shelter and adoption center. Their precise policy today is unknown. But Evan continues to do his work saving cats, even though no longer associated with the organization he founded. "I can get up to twenty calls a week these days," says Evan. "That could represent as many as a hundred animals. I simply cannot take in every cat that needs help, especially now that I no longer have an affiliation with C.A.T. What I can do is try my best to immediately find homes for them."

The Man Who Wouldn't Kill Cats

Cats come to Evan in every conceivable condition, some perfectly healthy, some drastically ill, most somewhere in between. The cuteness of a kitten is probably the most irresistible to a potential adopter, although some adult cats strike the right chord in someone's heart, and they too come in and go out the door to new homes. "Why should cats that many might consider 'undesirable' not also have an opportunity at a quality life, regardless of how much time they have left?" asks Evan. "There really is a tremendous reward in taking in these cats."

Every -ology

Evan has used every "ology" there is in the book – feline oncology, hematology, cytology, cardiology, dermatology, and on and on. The specialists list is as extensive for cats as it is for people and Evan makes certain his cats get the right treatment from the right practitioner, as their needs call for it. "I once spent $5,000 on one little kitty," says Evan, "and ended up adopting her out for $75. Was that a good use of my money, to take that kind of a loss? I believe the answer is 'yes' with every fiber of my heart and soul. Someone remarked to me after that particular cat that I didn't get much of a bang for my buck. My reply was that I get the biggest bang for my heart." Evan's dream was that this personal philosophy would always prevail at C.A.T. It was one of the saddest days in his life when he had to leave the organization he founded because he could no longer be certain that the shelter and adoption center would live up to his ideals.

Is There a Doctor in the House?

"A veterinarian's abilities vary," says Evan, "and if a regular vet doesn't have the capability to handle a given situation, I'll see to it that the cat gets seen by someone, usually a specialist, who has the knowledge and training the animal requires."

Two Legs Better Than None

It would not be feasible to put every story that Evan has about the cats he has rescued into one small book. There are some stories that stand out in his mind, and must be told. One of those involves a feline fellow named Oscar Peabody. Oscar was discovered by two young boys, in a bag inside a dumpster. The cat's owner was evidently unwilling to deal with Oscar's medical condition, for the cat still had on a harness, and was left to die in the closed garbage container. This was in the days before I built the hospital at C.A.T., so I called a local vet I worked with and told him about the cat's situation. We ferried Oscar over right away, and the vet called me to tell me that while bathing the cat, "the water turned blood red." He was absolutely infested with fleas. The really bad news was that Oscar Peabody's two hind legs were paralyzed. It began to become clear why his owner abandoned him. I scooped him up and took him to a specialist who performed spinal surgery on him. During his period of recuperation, the veterinarian specialist took Oscar home with her and gave him aqua therapy every day in her bathtub. As so often happens in these cases, the doctor fell in love with Oscar and adopted him. He lived a full life for another three or four years, in the loving care of someone who had enough heart to care for him. Why there are such polar opposites in the world of humans – one who can throw away an animal into a dumpster to die, another who gave him a great life for his remaining days – is a mystery of our species that I will never understand. What I do know is that I am continually on the lookout for people like that nurse, people who understand that, as it says in the Talmud, "to save one life is to save the world."

Animal Demographics

As mentioned, Evan continues to answer his cell phone and the animals he hears about through those calls become very personal to him. He receives calls from people – his collaborators – looking to find a home for not just cats, but also dogs, horses and many other types of critters. His reputation has spread throughout the region. Those with his cell phone number know that Evan does not know how to say 'no.' "My collaborator list is made up of dozens of people," says Evan. "I've traded cats for dogs, horses for ducks – whatever it takes to get a homeless animal a place to live. If they're alive and I can save their life, I'll get on the phone and spend the time to do it." Some of these collaborators' stories are included later in this book.

Give Until It Hurts

In 2006, Evan donated the entire building he had built in Sherwood, Oregon, to C.A.T. It was originally appraised at $2.5 million, and carried a $750,000 mortgage. Evan agreed to pay the mortgage for another two years with the organization taking on that responsibility thereafter. Yet C.A.T. has refused to take Evan off the mortgage. "I do miss the ability to take in any cat that someone calls me about," confesses Evan, "but I plan to reinvigorate my ability to take cats no one else cares about, once I get a new sanctuary up and running. Cats are God's greatest creatures. I honestly believe that. That makes each one of them my first priority."

Cats Come First

"The hospital was my heart," Evan says. "I learned about the care the cats were receiving by asking a lot of questions. Since the cats were my first and most important consideration, I asked questions to make certain they were getting the proper care. I followed a cat from the moment it came in our doors, up to and through its adoption. If it needed the care of a specialist, I wanted to have a specialist see the cat. Some of the sicker ones even ended up on my prayer list. I thank God every night, too, for allowing me the resources to help these cats. I plan to make excellent veterinary care a part of the new sanctuary, as well."

The Luck of the Draw

Not every community will be fortunate enough to find an Evan Kalik who is willing to underwrite an organization that can take care of cats. With the willingness to start small there is no reason why Evan's example cannot be adopted by cities and towns around the nation. "It is my dream that the sanctuary idea will spread," says Evan. "I'd like to see a wildfire of awareness spread from community to community across America, even around the world."

PART FOUR

Collaborators, Conspirators, Compatriots, and Cohorts

"Who can believe that there is no soul behind those luminous eyes!"

THEOPHILE GAUTIER

K EN HICK HAS BEEN A FRIEND AND CONFIDANT OF EVAN KALIK ALMOST FROM the moment they met. His support and guidance have been critical, and his business and organizational skills, as well as his unquenchable and uncompromising attitudes toward animal welfare, make his a voice that must be heard. Ken has six dogs, ten cats, and three birds, as well as a menagerie of other assorted animals. To say that Ken is an animal lover is like saying the ocean is wet and deep. It's as obvious as the cat hair on his couch.

Kindred Souls

Evan and I have the sort of relationship wherein we feel like we've known each other forever. Interestingly, neither of us can recall exactly when or how we met but we have always felt comfortable and completely compatible with regards to our attitudes about animals, so I guess it doesn't matter. Because when I met Evan, one thing was for clear from the very beginning. It was the meeting of kindred souls. He was doing what I was doing, only on a much bigger scale. I had an instant admiration for someone who had reached his stage in life, after achieving great success in business, who could have retired and whiled away his days but instead chose to devote all this time, energy and resources to helping other living beings. He could have sold the building that he gave to C.A.T. and added to his wealth but instead turned it over to become a facility that was dedicated to the welfare of cats. How much of his personal money he put into C.A.T., I don't know. There is no doubt that it has been a considerable amount, in the millions of dollars, since C.A.T. opened its doors in 1998. There is also no doubt in my mind that he will do what he can to build and maintain a new cat sanctuary. It's just that now, he needs assistance from others who are willing to help.

The Measure of a Man

My every instinct tells me that humans were put on the planet as caretakers, of each other and of our fellow creatures. Basically we have two choices: we can focus only on ourselves and the fulfillment of our desires, ignoring others or actively contributing to their suffering. This path measures success in terms of how big our bank account is and how many worldly goods we amass. The other choice beckons us to open wide our arms and hearts and try to take in as much of the world as possible. When we select this path, the rewards are endless and true fulfillment is possible. Our footprint will be measured not on what we have accumulated, but what we have given back.

No Self

What kept me involved for so long with the Cat Adoption Team is Evan's selfless passion for cats. Before I met him, my family and friends were rescuing all the cats we could, picking up strays that had been brought into Dove Lewis Emergency Animal Hospital in Portland, or anywhere they cropped up, which seemed to be everywhere. By "we" I mean my immediate family as well as many of the folks who work for me or with whom I have an association in everyday life. All have an open-hearted attitude towards their fellow creatures, including but not restricted to, cats.

All Species May Apply

We save horses at my sanctuary in Redmond, Oregon, and lots of other kinds of critters that come across our paths in need of a home. Hal, our office cat, is among those we have rescued, and he makes certain my operation runs smoothly. Counting Hal, I am the human companion of nine other felines, all of whom live at home, and all but two of which are special needs cats. I also have three ponds of rescued fish, along with four rescued birds – one lives in my office – and six dogs. I think my personal vet bill runs around $6,000 per month.

Animals, One And All

Some of the ways in which we treat animals are, in my opinion, criminal in nature. The factory farming of cows, poultry, pigs, and other food animals is nothing short of abject cruelty. We actually feed ourselves on their fear and mistreatment, making the consumption of such "food" unhealthy for us and deadly for the animals involved. We need to do a far better job of stewardship than how we handle that responsibility today.

An animal that is homeless is the direct result of human ignorance and lack of caring. Most of the cats that come our way are animals that someone has just dumped off and walked away from. A person makes a conscious decision to not do the responsible thing when they don't spay or neuter their animal, or breed animals in their basement with no regard for the animals, caring only about their own profitability. Many so-called "puppy mills" or the breeders of purebred cats generate so many animals that the owners end up euthanizing as many as two-thirds of the litters they breed into existence. There is no justification for killing an animal because they are "in the way" or otherwise an inconvenience.

Shouldering the Burden

These types of human insanity call for us to take responsibility for such animals and not to turn our backs on them. Animals are sentient. They experience love, fear, affection and a wide range of emotions and feelings that we cannot claim as strictly the province of human beings. They are not objects. They are living, breathing beings. It's best to remind ourselves from time to time that we too are animals and have much more in common with our fellow creatures than not. It is beyond arrogance to assume that we can do what we wish with non-human animals, even if the rationale is that we're saving human lives. I work closely with Oregon Health & Science University in an effort to install simulators that allow medical students to perform even the most sophisticated surgical procedures without maiming or killing animal test subjects. The time to stop torturing animals in our "medical experiments" is long past due.

Thinking Thrift

Now that Evan is disassociated with C.A.T., and moves forward with his plans for a cat sanctuary, he will find it almost impossible to function on donations alone. Some form of earned income, like a Thrift Shop, can help ensure that operating capital is always streaming into the organization's bank account. Grant money is available from such companies as PetCo and PetSmart, as well as numerous foundations. It takes an experienced grant writer to ferret through the requirements that foundations have established in order to qualify for and to write a successful grant request. Endowments from the estates of high net worth individuals can also be an invaluable source of long-term income.

Planning the Plan

All of these components are the key ingredients to a workable business plan. An impassioned love of cats is a bottom line that has to be backed up by a real world bottom line of dollars and cents. In that sense, a non-profit business has the same requirements as a for-profit enterprise. High profile charities attract to them affluent people who can help guarantee that they survive and thrive. More modest charities traditionally don't have big check-books to fall back on. Unfortunately, most animal welfare organizations fall into the latter category.

Just Say "Yes!"

I think actress and animal rights activist Gillian Anderson best captures the spirit of volunteerism when she writes the following.

Be of service. Whether you make yourself available to a friend or co-worker, or you make time every month to do volunteer work, there is nothing that harvests more of a feeling of empowerment than being of service to someone in need.

What I would add to that insight is that any animal welfare organization cannot exist without a dedicated cadre of volunteers. That reality creates its own special challenges. You can't call up a volunteer and tell them to report for duty at 8 o'clock tomorrow morning, or else. These people are sacrific-ing their time and energy to see that the organization's mission goes forward, and their voice must be heard whenever a concern arises among their ranks. That doesn't mean that a board of directors or the management team can allow the volunteers to run the organization, but it does mean that a very talented, energetic Volunteer Coordinator must keep the lines of communi-cation open between the volunteers and the rest of the organization.

Atta Boys and Girls

Volunteers must be recognized regularly for their work, through awards or other incentives, with frequent social gatherings like picnics or other casual get-togethers. They must be infused with a sense of mission and allowed to see how their efforts are vital to the organization's very survival. They must be made to know how deeply their volunteer work is appreciated.

"If a homeless cat could talk, it would probably say, 'Give me shelter, food, companionship and love, and I will be yours for life!'"

SUSAN EASTERLY

Is one's love for animals learned or is it something with which one is born? **Cindy Morrison** tends to think it is the latter. Her earliest memories are of feeling connected to her fellow creatures, knowing instinctively that it is part of our responsibility to care for one another as the need arises. Growing up in San Francisco, she found it was always easiest for her to have a cat rather than a dog. For Cindy, there is always a sense of comfort and rightness associated with the presence of a cat. Conversely, Cindy feels that a house is empty without a cat. She currently has one cat that was born blind, ironically named Iris, rescued from sure euthanasia ten years ago.

Encounter of the First Kind

As with countless others, I met Evan Kalik when I volunteered at the Cat Adoption Team. My entrée to that world came in 1999 after I read an article about Evan in the *Sherwood Gazette*. I remember being impressed from the first moment I met him with his kindness and encouragement. My first assignment was as a caregiver to the cats. Eventually, I took the job nobody wants as intake coordinator, a series of responsibilities many recognize as the most challenging position at the shelter. Blindly stumbling my way the first year through a position for which I had no experience, I managed to raise $25,000 for the shelter. Another year, I brought in $40,000. All the donations involved the slow process of talking about the shelter with people who brought cats into the shelter, encouraging them to open their hearts and wallets to the work being accomplished there. My logic was simple: the person needed to find a place for their cat, and we needed support to offer that sort of service. As the economic lives of people have taken a sharp downturn, more and more cats needed help, with less and less donations made available to provide it.

The Power of Nature

Hurricane Katrina, the deadliest and most destructive hurricane of the 2005 Atlantic hurricane season, gave Evan and C.A.T. an opportunity to shine. Evan was one of the first people to respond to the needs of pets in peril because of Katrina, and he asked me to spearhead the effort. Through Flight Services at American Airlines, I hooked up with another flight attendant who wanted to help and flew to Dallas, Texas, to meet with her. We drove fourteen hours straight through to Tylertown, Mississippi, headquarters of the Humane Society of Louisiana. We volunteered there for three days, sleeping at night in the car. We worked with people from all walks of life from every conceivable place across the United States who had come to help. Hurricane Katrina was history but another storm, Hurricane Rita, was bearing down on the region and we were advised to leave after only a few days. I grabbed a dog and a cat and we headed out, ending up at a shelter in Dallas that was taking in more Katrina-stranded cats than they could hold. This was an opening for us to rescue cats by sending them back to Portland. A private jet was secured and flew in from Atlanta, Georgia, to Dallas. We loaded the plane up with 51 cats, making one stop on the way home to pick up some PetSmart volunteers also trying to make their way back to Portland. Those volunteers gave our traveling kitties an examination to see how they were holding up. Then we were airborne again.

Home Again, Home Again

Upon our return to Portland, while I was the first one to deplane a cat, the local news media was more anxious to interview anyone with a white coat – the veterinarians who had volunteered to travel to New Orleans and other places where Hurricane Katrina had hit. The morning after our return, there was a segment about our trip on a local station, and Evan made certain I was called in for an interview. He was the one who actually put up the resources to bring back as many cats as we could but, ever self-effacing, he wasn't interested in publicity. He wanted people to hear directly from those who experienced the trip, and he wanted folks to know that even if you're not a medical professional, you have something to offer as an ordinary volunteer. Thus he made certain I was interviewed.

No Excuses

The idea of returning or otherwise abandoning an animal companion does not compute for me. These animals are part of our family. While I recognize the economic or logistical circumstances sometimes arise that make it challenging to keep a family together, I have no patience for those who want to rid themselves of their responsibilities because a cat no longer matches the furniture or some other equally absurd reason for turning their backs on their companions. Beyond the thoughtlessness and selfishness of such decisions, where is the heart energy, the compassion that we are here to demonstrate to one another?

Doing The Right Thing

No one can be forced to do the right thing, so there will always be a need for shelters and adoption centers. The plans Evan has for a cat sanctuary are another stopgap measure that will be a welcome addition to our community. At the same time, it will not be enough. My experience teaches me that people will generally take the easiest way out when it comes to getting rid of a no longer convenient animal companion, and Evan's sanctuary will no doubt fill up right away. Still, at least some cats will find refuge, and that is a very good thing.

"As anyone who has ever been around a cat for any length of time well knows, cats have enormous patience with the limitations of the human kind."

CLEVELAND AMORY

Kenny's Kats

Kenny-Cyr Rumble and Evan Kalik make perfect allies, both embracing the idea that cats have as much right to live on this planet as any other creature. More than that, they both believe that it is their personal mission and responsibility to provide safe haven for cats that might otherwise be discarded by humanity. This single idea has brought them into an alliance that is working very well for the felines that cross their respective paths.

The Beginning

When I was a little girl my mother bred Siamese cats. I've since learned how harmful cat breeding can be, but that experience of always having cats in the house is what led to my lifelong passion for cats. My mother's dad, my grandpa, hated cats so my mother grew up without them and, I guess, was making up for lost time. When she finally decided to discontinue her breeding business, she kept one last cat for our household, and that cat, Jasmine, chose me as her companion. I was about 9 years old, and she lived to be just three months shy of her 20th birthday. That was my first cat, and from that moment on, I haven't been without cats in my life.

Oregon Cats

When my family moved to Oregon, my husband and I decided that I would be a stay-at-home mom to tend to the upbringing of our troublesome daughter. That decision also gave me more time to devote to other activities.

I became a volunteer for several different non-profit organizations, including the Feral Cat Coalition of Oregon. I coordinated their plant sales, one of the primary ways they raised operational funds. It was a natural activity for me since I have a green thumb and love to garden. I put my marketing skills to work and the sale of plants grew way beyond the small scale that it was before I got there. It got to a point where I had to rent a truck to pick up all the plants we had growing in greenhouses around the city. In the largest sale in their history as an organization, we raised $8,500 in a two-day period. That may not sound spectacular, but it was a lot of plants, selling plants between 25 cents and $25, and the Coalition really needed the operating capital. The venture became so successful that I started a nursery, but parted ways with the Feral Cat Coalition because they didn't want to own a nursery, feeling that running it would detract from the primary mission – saving feral cats.

POPPA Founded

I next started an organization called POPPA – the Pet Over-Population Prevention Advocates (poppainc.org/index.shtml), which by 2010 was directly responsible for funding 18,532 spay and neuter surgeries throughout the State of Oregon since its inception in September 2001. I used the profits from the nursery to nurture POPPA and its spay/neuter mission. Our goal was to provide this service to companion cats, in order to not conflict with the Feral Cat Coalition's mission. We also wanted to avoid becoming a cat shelter that would dilute the successful adoption work being done by places like the Cat Adoption Team that Evan Kalik founded.

For Non-Human Animals Only

Coincidental with the founding of POPPA, Evan built a hospital within C.A.T. The two organizations formed a partnership to expand a spay/neuter program. I had met Evan at various C.A.T. functions, and I had fostered a couple of litters of kittens that came through C.A.T.'s doors, but he and I had no personal working relationship at first. At one point, I even applied for the position of executive director at C.A.T. but did not get the job. Evan, meanwhile, had also been trying for two years to get some kind of spay/neuter effort going that would be sponsored by Yamhill County government, to no avail. At one of the many concerned citizen meetings held by Yamhill County Commissioner Mary Stern, Evan and I began a relationship after I initiated a $10,000 donation from POPPA toward a spay/neuter effort in the county, which otherwise has no publicly funded program to benefit the welfare of cats, stray, feral, or otherwise.

Closing the Plant Plant

Eventually, in 2008, I decided to close down the nursery. At that time, I had only seven cats in my care. Now that I was freed up from the responsibilities associated with the nursery, as well as those that took up a great deal of my time fundraising for POPPA, my fostering activity started to ramp up. It is only natural that fostering leads to an increased personal cat population, at least for me. There are so many unadoptable cats – older ones, ailing ones, and problem behavior ones – so the quotient of cats under my care began to grow. I cannot bear the idea of these beautiful animals spending their remaining years in a cage, so every time I come across one, I swoop it up. Then, of course, I develop a relationship with each one and from that point on, I'm not going to turn them over to a shelter or otherwise discard them. This is what led to a parting of the ways between Evan and C.A.T., as more and more of those types of cats came back to C.A.T. and the pressure grew for them to dispose of unwanted cats. Evan finds euthanasia as intolerable a solution as I, for cats that still have plenty of life and love in them. There was a lot of loose talk in our politics at one point about "death panels" getting rid of grandmother and granddad, and Evan and I were not going to stand aside and let that happen to cats that we have anything to say about. I have no idea what C.A.T. decided in this regard. I can only hope they found a more compassionate solution that snuffing out the lives of "inconvenient" cats.

Green Lights, Blue Skies

The number of cats in my life grew. Rapidly. I live in a large home and felt that I could handle the increased feline population just fine. The cats with behavioral problems – mostly those that urinated indiscriminately – had my garage all to themselves with a door that allowed them to come and go, except at night when I locked them in for their own safety. I regularly hosed down the garage for purposes of hygiene. The other cats stayed in the house with me. None of the neighbors complained. I had an agreement with them that if they found any evidence of my babies in their yard, they were to let me know and I would rapidly remove unwanted cat waste. I did plenty of that, always willing to keep my word so there would be no neighborhood resistance to the presence of the many cats on my property. All seemed well.

Red Lights, Gray Skies

At some point, right around fourteen cats coming and going from my garage, some neighbors started developing attitude. By the time I got to seventy cats – that's right, seventy – someone called the county animal control authorities to report that I was harboring many more than the four the county allows for one domicile. I had to move the cats out or move out with my cats within two weeks in order to be in compliance with the ordinance. I began what I can only describe as a desperate search for an answer.

White Knight

That's when Evan became our savior. Two of my friends recommended I take my plight to him. When I called and explained my dilemma, he didn't hesitate to offer me a solution. He told me to come over that very day to check out a space he had found, a barn far enough away from any town that my cats would not disturb anyone. It turned out to be ideal. The upper portion of the barn is huge. As of this writing, there are eighty-eight cats inhabiting the space. Evan, unable to ever say "no" to a cat that needs a home, has added to our little cat city, and why not? How could I say no to the person who has so generously provided a haven for my original brood.

The Cat's Meow

Most are free to roam about the barn, while some remain caged for initial periods of adjustment, especially those cats that are not accustomed to a multiple cat environment. The responsibility is huge, but I love doing it – all the feeding, litter box emptying, medicating and, mostly importantly of all, the loving and nurturing. I spend, on average, two to four hours a day involved in these tasks. Occasionally, I will sleep on a cot overnight, just to provide the cats with a little more human companionship. It costs me, on average, $200 a week to feed the community of Kenny's Cats. For a time, I was spending $300 a month on cat litter, but recently found a less expensive brand, a product that dissolves into sawdust and can be deposited into a "green waste" bin.

Life's Ebb and Flow

A few of my babies have died, the natural consequence of any large population, and I've managed to find adoptive homes for some. Until either of those occurrences, my cats are safe from the wiles of the out-of-doors, including traffic and predators. Their personalities run the spectrum, as it is with any collection of living beings. Some are standoffish – especially the feral cats – and want me and other people (sometimes other cats, too) to leave them be. Others are variously affectionate and like to have that affection given back to them. You learn with cats to allow them to set the tone for the relationship.

The Mystery of It All

What precisely it is that draws me to these mysterious creatures, I can only guess. They don't seem to have the same neediness as our canine companions. Dog people need to be needed. We cat people are less prone to needing the need, if that makes any sense. Dogs are amazing in that they seem to love everybody. Sure, there are dogs trained to not be so loving, to put it mildly, but generally speaking they slobber themselves over anyone who is willing to pet them. It is in the nature of a cat to give or withhold itself as it sees fit, and I love that about them. When they do decide to draw closer, usually because you have demonstrated to them that you are worthy of their trust, it makes it that much more precious. Just as with relationships between humans, trust is a major factor with cats. I sense that even the cats that wish to remain aloof appreciate the care I give them, and that is satisfying enough for me. They know who feeds them, and are grateful for it. The best approach I have discovered for drawing a cat into playfulness is the laser pointer. They find that little red dot irresistible! Even the feral cats participate in the playful chase, their hunter instinct apparently aroused by the illusive point of red light. The old world, analog string is also a sure bet to lure a line of cats running behind me to catch the string. The best part of my day is when I'm coming up the stairs of the barn and I hear the patter of little paws making their way to greet me.

The Man of the Hour

My husband has reluctantly agreed to allow up to ten cats in our house (hidden away from the neighbor's prying eyes.) He views ten cats as an easy to accept situation after having lived with upwards of seventy at one time. My goal is to eventually find another situation wherein I can have an office right adjacent to my cats. I do not view Evan's hospitality as open ended, although I feel certain he would allow us to remain as long as necessary. Evan has the deepest wellspring of love for animals, particularly, that I have ever encountered in another human being. He is a complete softie when it comes to helping an animal. All you have to do is plop a critter in need down in front of him and he finds it impossible to respond with anything other than kindness and generosity. Evan Kalik is a special soul. To me, he represents what the entire human race may someday be like – unable to turn away another sentient being that needs help. I know his ability to trust other people has been wounded by the hurtful turn of events at the Cat Adoption Team, but if there's an animal involved, he jumps up to help, no questions asked. Evan is a giver, not a taker.

Who Lives, Who Dies?

Anyone who speaks with Evan soon comes to know his basic philosophy about determining when a cat should be euthanized. Evan insists – and I agree with him – that there is no excuse for killing a cat that still has the gift of life within it, a gift that can be nourished even if the cat has a behavioral issue or is ill but treatable. My philosophy has always been the same. If someone adopts a cat from me and reaches a juncture where they can no longer care for that animal, they are welcome to bring the cat back to me, rather than abandoning it by the side of the road or turning it into a shelter that regularly euthanizes animals because they don't have room for them. I

COLLABORATORS, CONSPIRATORS, COMPATRIOTS, AND COHORTS

put a microchip on every cat I care for, and my name remains as a primary contact should the cat become lost or otherwise uncared for.

Safe Haven

In Evan's case, he has always held that once a C.A.T. cat, always a C.A.T. cat, which is why he wants so much to create a cat sanctuary for unwanted cats that he feels have every right to live. When we assume responsibility for the life of a cat, it is a lifetime commitment. The idea of creating a cat sanctuary has been a long time coming, and Evan is the sort of man who will make it happen despite all obstacles. I have pledged my willingness to work with him once the sanctuary is a reality, as long as spaying and neutering are at the top of the agenda. The problem of cat overpopulation is, I believe, at the center of so many of the heartbreaking stories we hear about abandoned and feral cats. If people lived up to their responsibility to spay/neuter their cats, the need for a sanctuary would be greatly diminished. Educational outreach on this issue is critically important, and I would envision that as a significant role the sanctuary also must play. Evan has assured me that he wants to establish a mobile spay/neuter clinic that could flexibly handle not only the sanctuary population, but other places around the area, too. Twice monthly, mobile, low-cost clinics could be set up in different towns throughout the region while, at the same time, providing that service to the cats that come into the sanctuary.

The Long and Winding Road

As a nation, the United States has made significant inroads in its understanding of the preciousness of our fellow creatures. Compared to most other countries on the planet, we are light years ahead in our treatment of other sentient beings. That being said, we have oceans of progress yet to be realized. The suffering of animals raised for food is immense. The treatment of our companion animals is quite a long distance from perfect. There is hope, I believe, because there are people on the planet like Evan Kalik. When he asked me to tell my story for this book, I hesitated because I maintain a low profile. Like Evan, I desire no reward or recognition for the work, the loving work, I do for animals, in my case and his, especially cats. When he told me that this book might help him in his goal of getting donations for his proposed cat sanctuary, I immediately said yes. A person does not have to devote themselves entirely to the task of helping animals to make a difference. I have seen through the years how the accumulation of enough small gifts can mount up to have a powerful impact. Literally every penny matters. Enough of them, and the safety, the very lives, of our fellow travelers on this Earth can take a dramatic turn for the better. I urge the reader not to assume their contribution, no matter how small, is insignificant. In the hands of a man like Evan Kalik, you can be certain that gift will go a very long way toward the alleviation of suffering.

"I love cats because I enjoy my home; and little by little, they become its visible soul."

JEAN COCTEAU

Jeanie Sloan is the co-founder and Director of Operations of Salem Friends of Felines. She feels that Evan Kalik's support was instrumental in assisting her and a group of like-minded friends getting their organization off the ground.

Salem Friends of Felines

It all started with an idea that I and six others had in the fall of 2003 to create some kind of spay and neuter clinic for cats in the Salem, Oregon, area. Three of the original Gang of Seven and I are still involved. The others have dropped out for a variety of different reasons. Each of us knew one another through our common volunteerism with the Salem Wildlife Rehabilitation organization. I am one of the original board members of Salem Friends of Felines, and currently am one of only two employees in an otherwise volunteer-based organization. We try not to have more than forty-five cats in the house at one time. That can be a difficult goal to maintain, as the economy has slowed the number of adoptions, on average. We also have a large number of special needs cats that are more difficult to place – cats with certain behavioral problems or with communicable diseases like feline AIDS and feline leukemia.

Meeting Evan Kalik

The other co-founders and I are all like-minded in two ways – we felt that our lives were not complete unless we were being of assistance to others, particularly animals, and we all loved cats in particular and knew the lack of any facilities for cats in Salem was a growing problem. Two of our co-founders were on the board of directors at the Willamette Humane Society and had become increasingly unhappy with the rate at which cats were being euthanized. My mother was volunteering at the time at the Cat Adoption Team, and she spoke highly of Evan Kalik, suggesting we contact him for advice about how to get started.

Three Questions

When we met, we talked at length, but there were three questions about which he was especially interested in hearing our answers. "Do you have any money?" he asked. "No," was our answer. "Do you have a facility?" he wanted to know. Again, "no" was our unanimous reply. Finally, he wanted to know if we were in agreement with one another about the problem that required a solution, as well as if we shared a singular view of how the problem was going to get solved. To that, we could and did respond with a resounding, "Yes!" It was at that juncture that Evan decided to advise us as to how we could move forward. "Your first job," Evan told us, "is to raise some money."

Saving for the Cats

In April 2004, we received our designation as a not-for-profit 501(c)3 organization. Our first fundraiser was a garage sale that netted $500. Not a great "grubstake," but a start nonetheless. Ever so slowly we established a modest spay/neuter program. We still have that program in place. We give people a voucher with which a family pays a veterinarian $20 to perform the surgery, and we are billed for the rest. Not many vets came on board at first, but enough said yes to give us a chance to get going.

Turning a Corner

In June of that year, the local Humane Society moved out of their satellite adoption location at one of our Salem PetSmarts. Not wanting to allow this great opportunity to get in front of the public to slip away, we took the former Human Society space and spoke with Evan and asked again for his input. Evan offered to supply us with our first cats for adoption. He would let us keep $35 from each adoption, the balance of the adoption fee going to C.A.T. So it was that our first sixty cats came to us from C.A.T. The arrangement didn't last long because the people in Salem heard about us and suddenly there were cats jumping through our doors. A "hotline" that we established was also jumping off the hook. We began to set up our first foster homes. While we still didn't have a permanent home yet, we were in business.

Many Meows

Before we knew it, we were flooded with calls for assistance from people who needed help with their cats. The need was much larger than we had thought it was. We suddenly had plenty of cats, but the question remained: where do we put them? We really needed a space of our own. In the meantime, we used the PetSmart location as best we could. Every weekend we had special outreach campaigns to keep cats going out the door. Saturdays and Sundays were hopping, as fosters brought their cats into the PetSmart store. Carriers were piled high as we worked to find homes for their occupants. As is always the case in these sorts of situations, volunteers were critical to our success. If people don't show up to help – and it's that way today – the job doesn't get done.

Baling Wire and Duct Tape

We started out with nothing. Evan was generous with his personal finances to get C.A.T. going with a building and operating capital. We grew slowly, raising money as we went along with a variety of small fundraisers. It took us a couple of years to do it, but we eventually had $75,000 in the bank, by the fall of 2006. We started a serious search for a facility and found the building we now rent at 980 Commercial Street Southeast in Salem, Oregon. It took us until March 2007 to get the space in shape for our purposes. Since we opened our doors, the demand has steadily increased each year. We do not have a hospital or clinic but have formed a partnership with Willamette Valley Animal Hospital. They send a veterinarian to us for a half day every week to treat our cats.

The Virtue of Thrift

We knew we needed a more steady income than we could garner from adoptions and the idea of a Thrift Store seemed the way to go after exploring how it has worked for other animal welfare organizations. A rescue center in Florence, Oregon, had been having wonderful success with their

Thrift Store and we toured their facility in order to get some ideas how to run our own operation. Our assumptions about the profitability potential of a Thrift Store have proven true, for our modest sized store brings in an average of $7,000 per month. Without that revenue, we could not survive. Our adoption program costs us between $6,000 and $8,000 per month. Without the store, there would be no longstanding adoption center here. For the rest of our needs, we rely completely on the kindness of donors. Our adoption fees are low, but we have to maintain them in order to remain competitive with the Willamette Humane Society, which offers all their cats for an adoption fee of $45. We supplement our income from donations received after we send out a quarterly newsletter, as well as an annual dinner – Paws and Purr-sonality.

Cats on Deck

Most Thrift Stores set up for animal welfare don't have any animals on site, the presumption being that people coming to such a store are looking for bargains, not animals. Because we needed to consolidate our operation for the sake of keeping overhead as low as possible, we do have our adoption center in the same location as our store. Other organizations have been imitating us because it appears that sometimes people do come for bargains but can't resist taking a cat home once they see them. Additionally, many people who come to the store don't leave with a cat, but seeing them on site turns them into supporters who are willing to make donations to help the cats. That sentiment has led often to people bringing in items we can feature in the Thrift Store. They want to help the cats, and that's their way of giving support.

Cats Rule Cat Rules

We normally ask that adopters keep their cats indoors. We sometimes waive that requirement after interviewing the adopter. Usually the person has to live on a piece of property large enough to accommodate an outdoor/indoor cat, located away from busy streets and highways. Sometimes the cat itself will lead us to granting an exception. If a cat comes to us that has been accustomed to the outdoors, it may be near impossible to expect them to acclimate to an indoor only environment. Such cats will never be content to remain inside a house or apartment. They want out! This raises the quality of life versus the quantity of life issue. Is it better for a cat to have a long, unhappy life either in a cage or trapped in a building if it doesn't want to be there, or to have a shorter life span living with the outdoor freedom it craves? We would prefer to have all our kitties safely indoors, but some of them simply do not want this kind of life. A collar and a microchip are good backup systems to let others know the cat is owned, and by whom, should it wander too far from home.

Special Needs Cats

Every shelter/adoption center eventually runs across the situation wherein there are many "special needs" cats clogging the adoption pipeline. FIV and leukemia cats, cats with behavioral problems like inappropriate urination, and older cats – these are all more difficult to find homes for. We have a Special Needs page on our web site that asks for the kind of special people needed with a large enough heart to give such cats a home. We have lowered the adoption fee for such cats to $25. In essence, we're giving them away. In addition to more heart space, adopters of these kinds of cats need to under-stand and be willing to accommodate the particular needs of an individual cat. Here at the shelter, for example, we have a three-legged cat that has a difficult time negotiating herself into a litter box and often pees just outside the box. We place a clean towel around the box each day on a tiled floor, and the problem is resolved. We wash a lot of towels, but it keeps us from having to euthanize the cat. These cats require us to educate the public about dealing with many different kinds of issues. While they are at the shelter, we get them out of their cages and into roaming rooms as feasible because, as mentioned, we want a cat to have a good quality of life as well as a long life.

Volunteer Value

We have many people who assist us as volunteers. One woman who is a law professor at Willamette University comes in every day to groom and pet as many cats as she can squeeze into one visit. It's her way of unwind-ing and connecting with the animals. Another woman comes by and puts a cat or two on a leash and walks them around the store. Without people such as these, we wouldn't have enough hands to go around. Volunteers are literally the lifeblood of our organization, since we only have two paid staff members, including me. I end up volunteering time far beyond the boundaries of my small paycheck. A volunteer does our bookwork for us. Every board member contributes beyond their service on the board. All of them are fosters. All told, there are about 110 highly motivated, very dedicated volunteers at Salem Friends of Felines. Our overhead is almost ridiculously low because we want every dollar that we can find to go towards the welfare of our cats.

Then There's the Why

My sense is that everyone is either born with an innate sense of connection to other animals, or they're not. Perhaps it can be learned but I still think that the learning builds on a deep love and devotion someone either possesses instinctively as a primary aspect of their spiritual life, or they do not. I feel sorry for those who are not driven by this desire. In my case, I was always the odd person out in our family, the one who goes to the home of a relative who has found a stray cat and takes the cat. It was an awakening for me when I met the other ladies who started this organization. Suddenly I realized there were kindred souls in the world, people who felt as passionately about animals as did I. "Wow!" I thought. "I'm not weird or crazy!" Or, if I am, there are at least other weird, crazy people with whom I can share this common love of God's creatures.

Best Friends

Several years ago, Best Friends held a conference in Portland and my friends and I attended. Michael Mountain, a co-founder of that organization, was the featured speaker at a conference dinner one night. He spoke of this very issue, that over time there are people who get together with like minds regarding the welfare of our fellow species on this earth. We realize we have this connection, he told us, and we realize that it's quite all right. For me, the feelings are all pervasive. I deplore how our farm animals are treated. I mourn the loss of habitat for the planet's wildlife due to human overpopulation and pollution.

One Cat at a Time

Sometimes the sheer scope of the problems we face seems overwhelming. How will I find a home for this cat or that cat? Where will next month's operating expenses come from? Are we really making any headway with our spay/neuter programs? These and scores of other questions go bouncing around inside my head. Then I look down at a cat sleeping peacefully on her bed, or scratch the chin of a cat that has come up and rubbed its head against mine. At such moments, it is all clear to me. I am here to help the cats, who help me by keeping me grounded. There is only one way to accomplish this, and that is to focus on one cat at a time. Salem Friends of Felines has a saying we use on our newsletters: *Rescuing one cat may not change the world, but for that one cat, the whole world will change.* Remembering that gets me out of bed every morning. The most important factor for us is to keep everyone "on the same page," as the saying goes. If a disagreement arises, we all remind ourselves that it is best to keep egos in check and to concentrate on why we are here – to help the cats that would otherwise have no one.

The Eternal Face

At the time when Salem Friends of Felines was just getting under way, I volunteered at the Oregon Wildcat Haven near Sherwood, Oregon. Here larger cats of many varieties find sanctuary – bobcats, mountain lions, and the like. It's not open to the public because of restrictions placed on them by the government, but volunteers keep them afloat as well. Cleaning enclosures and having bobcats rub against my leg struck me at the deepest level of my spirit. It was like no experience I have ever had while in a church. Staring back into the eyes of that bobcat was, for me, like looking into the face of God.

"How nice it is to think that feline dreams, like our own, are painted with creative brush strokes from time to time. Perhaps my cats and I even share the same dream: a world where all kittens are wanted and loved, and where every cat has a safe, warm place to sleep and to dream."

BARBARA L. DIAMOND

Gary Nelson and **Diane Dennis** are the founders of the Kittyhawk Cat Sanctuary. There is no other cat sanctuary quite like the one they have in their home.

About the Manx cat, Wikipedia[2] has this to say:

> *The Manx (Manx: Kayt Manninagh or Stubbin) is a breed of cat with a naturally occurring mutation of the spine. This mutation shortens the tail, resulting in a range of tail lengths from normal to tail-less. Many Manx have a small "stub" of a tail, but Manx cats are best known as being entirely tail-less; this is the distinguishing characteristic of the breed and a cat body type genetic mutation. The Manx are said to be skilled hunters, known to take down larger prey even when they are young. They are often sought by farmers with rodent problems.*

About Manx syndrome, the article continues:

> *"Manx Syndrome" is a colloquial name given to the condition which results when the mutant tailless gene shortens the spine too much. It can seriously damage the spinal cord and the nerves causing spina bifida as well as problems with the bowels, bladder, and digestion. Some live for only 3 years when affected with the disease. In one study it was shown to affect about 20% of Manx cats.*

---

2   (http://en.wikipedia.org/wiki/Manx_%28cat%29)

Here are observations from Gary and Diane, who devote their lives to cats with Manx syndrome, as well as other special needs cats.

Gary: We live south of Oregon City, Oregon. More than that, I'll demur with telling you because we are not open to the public and need to focus all our attention on our cats' special needs.

I've been a cat person since I was a kid. If you have to ask someone why they are "a cat person," you'll never know. It is one of those matters understood at the deepest of levels or not understood at all. From the cat's side of the equation, if a cat likes you, it's not because you're feeding her. He's not liking you because he thinks he needs to cultivate your goodwill, either. When a cat likes you, it likes you because it likes you. Conversely, if a cat doesn't like you, forget about trying to win him or her over. Maybe someday if they feel like it, they'll decide to change their attitude toward you.

When I went to college, I became temporarily cat-less. After graduation, my sister was serving in Moscow, USSR, in the Diplomatic Corps and asked me to take care of her cat, Frank, while she was gone. I agreed to do so. Diane and I were living side-by-side in a duplex.

Diane: I'm a more recent convert. I had never had a cat until Frank came into my life. I was having a mouse problem on my side of the duplex, and Gary and I decided to go to a hockey game and leave Frank in my place with all the cupboard doors open. When we arrived home, Frank was sitting right in front of the door. He backed around the edge of the couch, picked up a dead mouse and laid it out on the floor for me to inspect. I was stunned, amazed, and forever a cat devotee. What I have come to love most about cats is their fierce independence.

Gary: Cats are extraordinary survivors. The equation has become unbalanced because of man. We have destroyed or populated so much of the world that cats and many other species are in peril.

Diane: Most of us are city dwellers now, so we don't need cats as mousers as we did for so many thousands of years. At the same time, people who keep cats as pets often do not take responsibility for their obligations to a living creature. The population of cats has exploded because of our irresponsibility.

Gary and I got serious about our involvement with cats when we took on the care of a feral and abandoned cat colony at Clackamas Community College. It had become a prime dumping ground for people who wanted to get rid of their cats. I remember one of our first cats on campus, Bobby, had apparently been dumped by someone who decided they didn't want him anymore. He walked up to me and as much as said, "Oh! Thank God you're here! I didn't think I'd ever find somebody to take care of me again!" It was fairly easy to find a home for Bobby because he was already tame.

Gary: I had read about England's cat colonies that were well cared for by law. It occurred to me to follow the Brits' example, after being encouraged to so do by a friend of ours, Virginia Myrick, another faculty member. We initiated the Clackamas Community College Campus Cat Colony Club – the seven C's – in the early 1990s. A few years later, that led us to create our own endeavor, the Kittyhawk Cat Sanctuary.

Diane: At the campus, we set up traps that wouldn't harm the cats in order to catch them for spaying and neutering. People create a bigger problem when they feed feral cats without trapping them and having them "fixed." The problem literally multiplies. We also set up feeding stations for the cats once we introduced them back into the colony. That re-introduction came only after we made an effort to place the cat in a good home first. We tried to find foster homes for kittens until we could find them a permanent home.

Gary: A great deal of volunteer effort went into the project, way beyond what just the two of us could have accomplished. I taught music at the college and, as a faculty member, I took primary responsibility as the club advisor, which gave the club standing on the campus as a legitimate enterprise. The cats became, in essence, campus property, giving us the legal right to protect them from the kinds of people who enjoy harming animals, particularly cats and dogs. We had the ability to raise funds and we plugged into the goodwill that existed among many of the students and other faculty members.

Diane: The project received additional legitimacy and momentum from a clinic held on the campus sponsored by the Feral Cat Coalition of Oregon.

Gary: The theory was that as an extension of a public college, we could accept donations for the colony. Veterinarians did give us discounts, and we had some modest results with fundraisers. In fact, however, we bankrolled virtually all of the project, and I'll guess that I've spent a couple of hundred thousand dollars on cats over the last twenty-five years, including our own sanctuary.

Frank, the cat that got all this started, disappeared one day. In an effort to find him, we found all sorts of homeless cats roaming about. Being not disposed to allowing harm to come to them, our personal cat crew grew. The gang grew to somewhere in the neighborhood of forty cats, making it apparent that we were in need of more space. We moved to a piece of land that had seventeen acres. That's how Kittyhawk Cat Sanctuary was born.

Diane: We wanted to create a non-profit 501(c)3 organization but there were too many hoops to jump through for our taste. The result is that we don't have the same sort of strictures on us about where money comes from that folks do who have a not-for-profit designation.

Gary: I'd rather we paid for it ourselves so we could move ahead as we saw fit. We still get a great deal of assistance from people like Evan Kalik. Steve Milner, DVM, of Milner Veterinary Hospital in Oregon City has been helpful, in terms of giving us discounts for the cats' medical bills. Dr. Bob Benski at Oregon City Veterinary Clinic has also been very kind in this regard.

Our sanctuary is run with a strictly "no kill" philosophy. Most, if not all, of our cats are of the kind that most people would view as candidates for euthanasia.

Diane: Our sanctuary is essentially private, at our house. People kindly offer to clean cat cages and the like, but we're happy to do the work ourselves. We also don't want to gain the reputation as a place to drop your cat off on our property.

At first, we focused our energies mostly on feral cats. With 2,000 square feet of fenced-in outdoor space, the site was perfect for that. Gradually we began concentrating on cats with chronic medical problems, like FIV and leukemia, feral or not. In 2001, Evan called and asked us to take two cats, one of which we still have named Armstrong, and that's how our association began with Evan. Armstrong is a Manx with the Manx syndrome symptoms of a lack of bowel and bladder control.

Gary: Over the past few years, we have turned our attention almost exclusively to Manx cats with severe genetic abnormalities. Most need to have their bowels and bladders expressed and some require diapers. We've decided to specialize in the care of these wonderful cats and phase out taking any other cats.

Diane: No one else we know of takes care of these types of cats. Just about anyone else would have them put down.

Gary: That's because nobody wants to spend three hours a day expressing urine and feces and changing cat diapers. We happen to find great purpose in offering this help to these cats, who express their gratitude to us in many different ways.

Diane: Breeders don't take into account that when they deliberately breed the Manx to have no tail, they are creating some cats with a birth defect. One in six in every litter, on average, is born dead. For those that live, some develop these problems in passing waste materials, as well as other potential deformities such as paralyzed hindquarters and malformed internal organs. There are drugs that can assist the cats in dealing with these challenges but as with all drugs, there are side effects. We do the process manually twice a day.

Gary: When we started years ago we had as many as 250 cats at one time. Today we have about thirty cats that require lots of attention and care each day. It might seem to some that what we do is heroic, but I reject that. It is we who are the winners. Or to put it another way, we feel that the rewards we get in return for providing these animals with a good quality of life far outweighs any inconvenience to us.

Diane: Absolutely. We deeply love and admire these cats. I'd wager that there are other people who would be willing to do what we do but they don't know about the need, especially if we could tell them about what they get in return, although it's difficult to find the right words to describe it.

Gary: Without people willing to do this, these cats would be dead. Period. Our motivation isn't to receive accolades. It's to enjoy what we're doing, to see the love in a cat's eyes when it knows you're keeping it alive and loving it to the bone. We do know of others who take in cats with terminal illnesses or other drastic health problems. They all do it because they truly want to. Anyone who has ever cared for a loved one in their family that is physically or mentally handicapped knows precisely to what I refer when I talk about the rewards. Like such people, our cats forge ahead with dignity and courage in the face of terrible odds.

Diane: We can learn from our little friends. They don't complain or whine about their situation. Instead they revel in life, squeezing every bit of enjoyment out of existence that they can.

Gary: Jessie, one of our cats, grew accustomed to Diane taking care of his elimination problems. When Diane went away for a short time, I took over those duties. Immediately, I noticed a difference in our relationship. Jessie was definitely aware that she was now in my care, and our friendship deepened. I could see evidence that she felt closer to me.

Diane: Another of our cats, Quincy, found a sick kitten outside and made it his business to hang around that baby until its health was restored. Quincy consistently, repeatedly, exhibited that sort of nurturing attitude toward other ill cats that came our way. Who can doubt, when they witness that sort of behavior, that these animals have rich emotional lives?

Gary: One final note on this idea of people who do what appears to others as extraordinary being heroes. To me, Evan Kalik is indeed a hero. Evan has accomplished more to save cats' lives and to improve the quality of their lives than Diane and I could ever dream of doing ourselves. He doesn't believe in sitting around and philosophizing about helping animals. He believes you find a way to move forward and you get up right away and take action. When Hurricane Katrina devastated the Gulf Coast, he arranged to have a bunch of stranded cats flown to Oregon and put under the care of C.A.T. That is taking action! As with other people we've mentioned, including ourselves, no one is doing this for fame or glory. We're in it for the sake of the cats.

Diane: You have to believe strongly enough that your good intentions will garner the support you need to achieve your goal. Just get going, and the resources will appear. Word gets around within the animal welfare community and people will come into your life who can help and advise you.

Gary: In most instances, nothing is going to happen unless you decide to do it. Inertia and inaction are the great enemies. Don't wait for someone else to come along. Take action and help as many cats are you can.

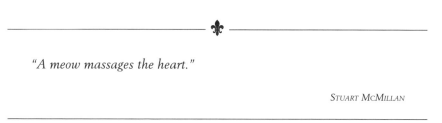

"A meow massages the heart."

STUART MCMILLAN

Linda Budilowsky, another lifelong cat aficionado who lives in Portland, Oregon, has worked with Evan Kalik as a cat rescuing collaborator for many years. A onetime employee of the Waltham Pet Food company, she has had countless cats pass through her life, many of them presenting themselves to her by literally coming to her door. All of them ended up being better off for doing so.

Pyrrhic Victories

The life of the animal rescuer is not always crowned with victory. I recall an incident in which an elderly woman in an assisted living facility reached out to me for help with her cat. The animal was ill and the woman was not mobile enough to get her darling to a veterinarian. When told of the situation, Evan was, as usual, quite willing to do whatever he could to help the woman and her cat. When I solicited the assistance of the home's administration, they washed their hands of it all, saying it was not their responsibility to get involved. Enough back-and-forth negotiations went on to allow the cat to eventually become extremely ill and die as a consequence. It may have been the only time I have ever seen Evan truly angry. "That pisses me off!" he said to me on the phone in a voice strained with frustration.

Consciousness Evolution

If anything good came out of it all it is that the home's administrators have since been more sensitive to their elderly client/residents' animal companion needs. They have actually approached me about one situation or another that involves a resident's cat in need of medical care! Change comes slowly, and often only after a loss of life or some other unpleasantness. This seems to be the way our species finally becomes willing to embrace one reform or another. We don't get motivated until there is a tragedy to which we must respond. These sorts of occurrences are, fortunately, mixed in with the successful rescue operations, those that make the heartache of failures at least a little more tolerable.

In Memory of Harry

There was a period of time in years past that I spent a great deal of volunteer time at the Cat Adoption Team. What I recall most vividly about those days is Evan Kalik's absolute devotion to the cats, most particularly those with special needs and those who had become very ill or were injured. A cat that came into the hospital covered in roofing tar comes to mind. Evan was there early every morning with that cat uppermost in his mind. Sadly, the cat succumbed to his condition. I was devastated and wanted to do something that would honor the cat's brief existence. The first thing I did was give him a name – Harry. Then I had him cremated and brought his ashes home, setting them in a place of honor. To the non-cat lover, this probably seems ridiculous, but Evan completely understood. He has retained the cremated remains of many of the feline companions who have shared his home. Every living being must be acknowledged, no matter how brief or seemingly unimportant their time on earth. Harry will live in my memory for as long as I draw breath.

Tommy

On a more uplifting note, I also remember a cat rescue that unfolded during the winter of 2003. My neighbor knocked on my door one cold morning. "There's a kitty on our patio," she informed me, "and I don't know what to do." Her husband was allergic to cats and even though she had some already in her home, she couldn't burden her mate with yet another source of allergic unpleasantness. I, too, had what I deemed the maximum number of cats for which I could care. My neighbor and I devised a box, complete with insulation, into which the kitty could find some respite from the winter's chill. I took the kitty, whom we named Tommy in view of his Tom Cat status, to a vet clinic. There Tommy was diagnosed with herpes virus of the eyes. They refused to allow the cat to stay, fearing he would spread the virus to other cats in the facility. They relented up to a point, allowing the cat to remain in a back storage room. As you can imagine, the cat found this depressing and he stopped eating. I went every day to try and coax him into taking some nourishment. A fellow cat rescuer friend recommended that I take the stressed-out kitty to the North Portland Veterinary Hospital where the immensely compassionate and skilled Don McCoy, DVM, is the head veterinarian.

Excellence in Animal Medicine

Dr. McCoy is a superb diagnostician, and he quickly assessed Tommy as not having the herpes eye virus. He was immediately certain that Tommy suffered from a condition known as entropion, an inversion of the eyelids. Tommy's eyelids were turned inside out, with the eyelashes continually irritating the corneas of his eyes. As a consequence, he was nearly blind. He had already hit the average lifespan of a feral cat – three years – but somehow found his way to my neighbor's patio to find refuge. After an expensive surgery to correct his condition, Tommy was further diagnosed with feline leukemia. That's when Evan entered the picture. He contacted another of his collaborators, Diane Dennis, who has a place south of Oregon City, where she ministers to kitties like Tommy. Thanks to Diane, Tommy did not remain a homeless wanderer. I paid Diane a sort of reverse adoption fee of $500, and she took him in. He lived a full life for several years before passing away.

Won't You Be My Friend?

On another occasion involving a senior resident at a retirement home, an elderly woman called to seek help in finding a home for a Siamese cat she could no longer care for. I spoke with Evan about the situation and he put me in touch with Salem Friends of Felines. As the Universe would have it, a woman who had recently lost a Siamese cat was looking for another Siamese to care for, and we matched them up. The adopter didn't own a car, so she came up to Portland on the train to claim her new beauty. I love a happy ending!

Sanctuary

The fact that Evan is diving into the new venture of establishing a cat sanctuary is quite exciting, and has fired the imaginations of many within the cat rescue community in this region. Funds remain a big issue, and I urge anyone who can contribute to do so. When I think of the number of cats whose lives will be saved and cherished, it brings me a lot of happiness.

———

"Everything a cat is and does physically is to me beautiful, lovely, stimulating, soothing, attractive and an enchantment."

PAUL GALLICO, FROM AN HONORABLE CAT

Tammy Goddard was a long-time volunteer at the Cat Adoption Team. She has been a confidant and collaborator of Evan's for many years. She started with five cats of her own back in those days, but today will say only that now she and her husband have "many, many" cats and other animals, too. Residence in the rural environs near Sandy, Oregon, makes that lifestyle possible.

Meeting the Man

I met Evan not long after he opened the Cat Adoption Center, perhaps six months or so later in 1998. They were running a public service announcement on local television about the opening of a "no kill" cat shelter and that immediately got my attention. I offered my volunteer services, inspired by the dedication I saw that Evan and his wife Ardie brought to the operation. I cleaned a great many cages, and I'm very fast. I'll wager that I cleaned thirty or more cages a day, with Evan and Ardie right there cleaning with me. Getting involved in any of the adoptions wasn't for me. Like Evan, I would have been very particular about who was allowed to adopt a cat, simply because so many people start out with good intentions and then somewhere along the line forget about their responsibility to the living being they have taken into their care.

Excelsior

There have been so many opportunities for me to see Evan at his very best. He reminds me of a mountain climber who, when he stumbles, gets back up immediately and continues to move toward the heights. I often brought feral cats to him and he always welcomed the newcomers with open arms and a warm heart. His campaign to open a sanctuary that will care for, among others, feral kitties, is a wonderful idea. Feral cats lead a short life filled with struggle and fear. Having a respite at a sanctuary where they will be loved and cared for under Evan's kind supervision will be like going to heaven for them.

Countless Cats

In the course of my cat rescue activities, I also transported many a feline to adoption centers sponsored by PetSmart on behalf of C.A.T. My first inspiration, of course, was the cats. Seeing Evan frequently and watching him in action ran a close second. One of the less elevating factors in cat rescue is the number of irresponsible people who, for one reason or another, abandon their cat companions. I understand that financial setbacks can make the commitment to caring for the four-legged members of our families a challenge. There is, however, no excuse for dumping a cat by the roadside or killing the animal because it has become inconvenient. One of my goals has always been to educate people about the alternatives to such cold-hearted "solutions." Find a home for the cat, or bring it to a shelter where it can be adopted. Giving up and leaving a cat to fend for itself or snuffing out the animal's life are not acceptable. These are sentient beings, with deep emotional lives. I ask people to mentally put themselves in the cat's situation for a moment and to imagine being dumped off somewhere because you had become "inconvenient" to others. It is a terrible fate. I have rescued many a cat that has lived with an elderly person who finally reaches the stage where they can no longer care for themselves, much less an animal companion. Society doesn't ask for the elderly to stop living because of their age and infirmities. Cats, I strongly believe, should be extended the same compassion.

Miles to Go Before We Sleep

Spay/neuter programs have grown in size and scope in recent years but there still is an enormous cat population that can best be served through this strategy. Nature has provided cats with a prodigious capacity to breed, and a female will bear one litter after another unless we mercifully intervene. My husband and I have no children. Fortunately, he shares with me my love of cats and other animals. They have literally become the central focus of our world. It is delightful to have a human companion with whom I can share this passion. It is probably not the most skillful strategy to employ but I try not to keep track of the money I spend every month on food, litter, and other expenses, like veterinary care. Somehow, we always seem to have the resources that we needed. We have decided not to actively seek any more cats, even though they find a way to us whenever the Universe decides we are the ones who will answer the call as the situation arises. Living in the country makes life easier for everyone. We have insulated a large barn on our property, as well as adding a commercial heat source. This allows us to accommodate more of our little friends without having them take over our entire house, which is what used to happen before we moved away from the city. A fenced-off acre and a half gives the cats their natural outdoor experiences while confined in a way that keeps them safe from predators. For some, it's not enough and there is the occasional escapee. That too, is fine. If a cat wants total freedom that badly, we are not about to tell it that it has to stay.

Raccoon Face

One of the most vivid memories I have of Evan in action was the time he received a call about a cat that had gotten into a fight with a raccoon. He was told that half the cat's face had been torn away and, sure enough, when we found her the facial wounds she sported were quite severe. Here again, most people would have given up on this cat and had it euthanized. Not Evan. He insisted on providing the surgical repair the cat required. Every day, as the cat's condition slowly improved, he faithfully checked on the cat's condition until the day finally arrived where she was fit to begin life again. Evan is committed to saving cats' lives, and he puts that commitment into action every day of his life.

For the Love of Cats

Why this special attraction to cats? Most cat lovers will say the same, probably, as I in this regard. They are loving, deeply complex creatures who appreciate the kindness they are shown. Their independence, of course, is legendary and I appreciate that characteristic. Once you enter the rescue world, you are smitten for life. The need is so great and, as Evan will admit, we cannot save every cat that needs us. We can nonetheless, save as many as we possibly can.

"A cat's eyes are windows enabling us to see into another world."

IRISH LEGEND

There is a little country store in Scholls, Oregon, and most days if you stop in, you'll find **Linda Miller** behind the customer service counter. A cat rescuer of long standing, Linda is – like Evan Kalik – willing to do just about anything to take care of a cat that needs help.

Cat Dollars and Cents

It's often a challenge to do everything I want to do for cats that cross my path because of the limited income I make working at the store. Almost all of my salary goes for cat food and litter. My total take-home income is probably about $7,200 a year. First thing every paycheck, I head straight to Costco for food and litter. It's the vet bills that are hard to handle. Occasionally, people give me donations. Evan has been generous and kind and often helps me financially rather than see a cat suffer. There are periods where I can pay down the veterinarian bills, but they always manage to go back up, especially when a unique medical problem develops with one or more of my cats. A few years back, I had an incidence of fatty liver deposits appearing in four males that I rescued. I spent about $1,000 per cat getting them outfitted with feeding tubes and medication. That is a very large sum of money for someone in my position. It was a great deal of work, as well, with each cat requiring attention about every three hours for a number of weeks. I don't mind it at all when that happens. It keeps me focused, and the reward I get back when a cat recovers is immeasurable.

Thou Shalt Not Kill

Evan and Ardie Kalik are a special part of my life. When the need arises, I help Evan with work around his home in the country. What attracted me to Evan Kalik and the Cat Adoption Team from the beginning of my association with them is their "no kill" policy. People are gradually waking up to the cruelty involved in euthanizing cats just because they are inconvenient, and C.A.T. has been at the forefront of that movement in Oregon. If an animal has a chance to lead a normal life, even if it's FIV positive, diabetic, requires a special diet, or has feline leukemia, that cat should be allowed to live. Sure, it can be challenging to find a home that will take such a special needs cat, but there are people who are willing to do so, and we have to have the patience and persistence to find them.

The Gift

Most people probably have some story about how they came to love cats after being around them growing up. I think I was born with a love of all animals, cats in particular. I will rescue any of God's creatures that come my way, but my real passion is for cats. It is true that growing up on a farm gave me an early exposure to all sorts of animals, and my mother was a real cat lover. I learned about the importance of spaying and neutering from her early on in my life, how vital it is in achieving the goal of reducing the number of unwanted and homeless cats in the world.

Nine Lives Not Enough

Our cats lived mostly outdoors and because our family farm was situated on a busy highway, our cats were lucky if they made it to their second birthday. It was so hard for me when we lost a cat that way. I always became emotionally attached to each of them. It got to the point where my parents didn't want to tell me about the latest loss, but that was impossible because the cats were such a critical part of my everyday life. We finally moved further back away from the busy road, and our cats started living longer lives.

The Path of the Cat

Cats are simply amazing creatures, and I wish everyone had a deep appreciation for that fact. If they did, they wouldn't be drowning litters or dropping them off somewhere to fend for themselves. Once a cat bonds with you, they are literally your friend for life. Every cat that I have ever rescued has had its own way of letting me know how grateful they are for my efforts on their behalf. To say I have many cats is an understatement, which means that I get to see every possible variation of temperament. Some are like dogs, in that they follow me around and want my company every waking and sleeping moment. One of my cat companions leaps into my lap whenever I sit down and proceeds to demand immediate petting, leading to copious amounts of drooling – the cat, not me! She also loves to lick and knead. Some of my other cats are more of the traditionally stand-offish type, who let me know when they are ready for loving, always on their terms. It is this streak of feline independence that makes it so possible for cats to survive when they are abandoned. They are survivors to the core. That does not mean that every cat is going to fare well when left to its own devices. I have seen many cats on the brink of starvation after being dumped off by their human caretakers.

Abandonment

It seems that people are often ready to get rid of a cat for even the slightest of behavioral reasons. It takes a while to get to know a cat, and since they aren't objects like a piece of furniture, it surprises me that so many of us reject a less than perfect cat before really getting to know it. At my home, the cattery has a cement floor, eliminating the problems that sometimes come up when there's a lot of carpeting in a house. I much prefer making our home accommodating to our cats than living in some picture perfect house that is without the love and companionship of cats.

What To Do With Kitty

Some of my cats – now numbering somewhere north of twenty in my cattery with another eight or so ferals outside – are so-called "problem" cats. There are ones that trust me completely and let me pick them up and brush them or trim their claws. If I take them to the vet, it's another story. They act like they are feral. I do have some biters and scratchers and some with inappropriate peeing problems, but with the way I have my cattery set up, they can still have a home and live out their lives. They have as much right to a life as any supposedly "normal" cat, and I don't mind dealing with their eccentricities.

Fidelis

It doesn't matter what the conditions – a great snowstorm or whatever – I always feed and water my cats, including some colonies of ferals that don't live near my home. During that snowstorm, I put on my snow boots and slung a backpack full of food and water over my shoulders to hike into the feral colonies I have adopted, to make certain they could survive. One recent rescue comes to mind. I took in a ten-year-old female who had been an indoor cat only all her life. Regardless of her home life, she acts feral – she won't let me touch her – but she is a beautiful animal and I am determined that someday she will let me get close to her. Her temperament evolved from the fact that the woman who owned her fed her but never touched her. So that cat never became accustomed to that kind of interaction with people. Does this mean she should be euthanized? I say definitely not. Another of my cats that I rescued acted completely feral when I first got her, but now she lets me pet her. They can heal, they can change, maybe not to a point where they will make an ideal house cat, but certainly enough to warrant a good quality of life for themselves. The issue comes down to trust. If an animal has been traumatized by humans, why should that animal trust any other person who comes along? It takes time, but that bond of trust can be reestablished.

Cat Classroom

Can people learn anything from cats? I know I have and continue to do so. Their survival skills are exceptional. I think it's fascinating that cats get many of the same ailments and diseases that we do, such as diabetes, AIDS, leukemia, and various types of cancer. Basically, they need love, shelter, and food, and that sounds a lot like us, too. I don't think it's a stretch to say that they know how to offer gratitude. My ferals hear my truck pull into the driveway, and they run out to greet me, talking away.

The Power of One

When animals have experienced abuse, they respond with their own forms of post-traumatic stress symptoms, also very much like people. We don't discard people when they have such conditions. Why would we even consider killing a cat that has already been through terrible emotional circumstances? Essentially, I persevere in the sometimes long process of trying to find a good home for a cat. My goal is to find homes for as many of the cats that I rescue as I can, but I'm picky where they go. Once they've been rescued from the streets I want to be certain that they are going into a forever home and aren't headed back to the streets again. I really don't have the time to walk people through the entire adoption process either. This is where my collaboration with Evan comes into play. He has helped me find many a home for many a cat. I can relax knowing that Evan is as obsessed with the cat's care as I am. I am a firm believer on indoor-only homes. There are some cats that perhaps are the exception, but all things considered, cats should live indoors where it's completely safe for them.

Learn and Let Live

Educating the public about cats is the key to solving the overpopulation problem. The farm country where I live is peopled with fine folks, but they don't always have the compassionate attitude I would like to see them adopt towards cats. Sometimes out here cats are viewed as simply a nuisance. There are enough shelters and clinics dedicated to the spaying and neutering process that it's just a question of getting the cats in for the surgery.

Depth of Feeling

Cats have a deep emotional life. My ability to state that flatly is from years of being around them and observing them. I had one cat that, whenever I didn't feel well, became concerned for me, rubbing around my legs meowing and letting me know that she was worried about me. How can a cat know such a thing? I don't understand the process. I know that it is real because I have experienced it again and again.

"Those that dislike cats will be carried to the cemetery in the rain."

DUTCH PROVERB

Dana Gilbert is convinced that her love of cats has always been a part of her being. She remembers the cat that the family got when she was about one year old that lived until Dana was twenty-one years old. She recalls a long and wonderful relationship with that very first cat in her life.

One Is All It Takes

My parents were very practical, seeing the care of animals as an unnecessary expense, so we only had the one. Still, because the neighbors never bothered to spay or neuter their cats, there were always plenty roaming around. I was constantly trying to save the unwanted puppies and kitties that kept showing up, performing that task without any help from my parents.

A Cat Lover's Shelter

Many shelters have a reputation for euthanizing animals they can't find homes for, so I stayed away from shelter work – until I heard about the Cat Adoption Team in 1998. I had rescued a kitty that wasn't getting along with the other cats in my home, but I didn't want to turn her into a shelter where she might be "put to sleep." She was a black cat, which there's no shortage of, and I couldn't find anyone to take her. I heard about this new place in Sherwood that had a "no kill" policy and I gave them a call. I think they had been in business perhaps a week. It was, as the saying goes, the beginning of a beautiful friendship. They asked, "When can you bring her in?" That doesn't happen very often.

Founder's End

When I went to C.A.T. and met Evan, I thought he was just another volunteer.

He had his sleeves rolled up and was as busy as any hands-on volunteer could be. We were cleaning cages and he was right in there with everybody else applying elbow grease. "How long have you been volunteering?" I asked him. "I started the place!" he said. He was completely inside one of those really large double cages, and all I could see was his backside. That was my introduction to Evan Kalik – his rear end sticking out of a cat cage. I remember how exhausted he and Ardie were at the end of a day after medicating all the cats that required it. We cleaned cages and litter boxes non-stop. We called the hand washing of dozens of litter boxes in the shelter's small bathroom "therapy." If you had grown tired of being around other people, it was a perfect therapeutic exercise, one that soon made you grateful to get back around people and away from the distinctive odor of cat pee.

Starting a Family

I remember that first year, Evan and I and one other fellow were cleaning up the last of the cages for the day. It was the beginning of the July 4th holiday weekend and Evan turned to us and said, "Would you like to come out to my house for a barbecue?" I was surprised and a little bit nervous, but who can turn down a kind offer like that? I'm sure if there had been ten people at the shelter working, he would have invited us all over. His entire family was there when we arrived including, of course, his wife Ardie, and they were so warm and welcoming to me. He continues to invite me to his home at least a couple of times a year, and since that first phone call Evan Kalik has become family to me.

Solace for the Dying

From my very first year with C.A.T., I became involved as a foster caregiver, bringing home moms and their kitties. I never had designs on providing hospice care. In fact, the idea frightened me. I didn't want to see cats dying. Then one day two brother cats came into the shelter after being rescued from abuse and neglect. They had been locked in a garage for an entire year and every now and again, when the home owner remembered them, he would throw some food into the garage for them. They were so emaciated. One was diagnosed with lung cancer and no one would take him home.

Evan turned to me and said, "Dana, what about you?" My response was probably too quick and too loud. "No!" I said. "I can't!"

Caring to the End

I couldn't deal with the fact that this cat probably only had a month or so to live. Then I put myself in the place of the cat. What would I need if I were dying? How would I feel if someone reached out to me to give me comfort in my last days? Of course, I took him. He lived for two months, and they were rich and full for both of us. He wasn't sick the entire time, and even gained a bit of weight. Suddenly one day, he couldn't breathe any longer, so I took him to C.A.T. where they mercifully euthanized him. I had given that cat a loving home during his final weeks on earth, and it proved to be a profound experience for both the cat and me. I am certain he was happy up till the end, and I certainly gained a great deal of joy giving myself to him at the time of his most critical need. Not to say it wasn't difficult. Saying goodbye was the heartbreaking experience I expected it to be. I cried for a week, but everything that preceded that made it worth it. I had become a convert and have been housing hospice cats ever since. For many of them, it is the first time in their lives that they have experienced safety, a steady diet, love, warmth, and comfort. How can I refuse them?

Cats Here, Cats There, Cats Everywhere

I have eight cats, seven of them from C.A.T. This is the natural result of my now serving as the Adult Foster Program Coordinator for the shelter. There are just a few people willing to provide hospice care for cats and I love every one of them! I am certain there are many others capable of offering the support dying cats need, but they have not yet made that leap to the place where they are willing to expose their hearts to the sort of loss associated with such work.

Feline Respite

The logic for Adult Foster Care is simple. Shelter life can be difficult, even for a healthy cat. The animals get depressed, just as a human would under such confining conditions. Other cats may need an interim time period to heal from a broken bone or other injury or illness. Getting cats out of the shelter environment gets them away from potential infections, in the same way that people are more subject to infections during long hospital stays. Adult Foster Care allows a cat a chance to heal and to be observed to see how they get along with other cats and/or with people, and to see what sort of permanent home would eventually be ideal for them.

The Way of the Cat

The Cat Adoption Team teaches several classes a month on Foster Care skills, including how to give injections, such as insulin, the proper techniques for giving IV fluids, and how to expel a cat's bladder. Some of it is less than glamorous work, but cats sometimes need specialized medical attention, just like people. When people speculate that they will become too attached to a cat to give it up, let me assure them that there are always more cats in need waiting at the shelter. If it's just impossible to say goodbye, there's always the option of giving the cat a permanent home!

Loving Without Conditions

It's said so often that it has become a cliché, but it's true that cats give unconditional love. Each one is very much an individual, and some may not express their love as well as others, depending on how abused or otherwise traumatized they have been before they find a loving home. They can teach us so much about perseverance and courage. Cats are smart and cute and great companions. What more could a human ask for? Evan has a huge heart in which he has made room for thousands of animals. He has saved the lives of so many cats. He could have done what many successful businessmen do and traveled around the world in his retirement years. Instead, he has dedicated his money, time, love, and other resources to cats.

PART FIVE

Sanctuary

"Whoever has compassion for other creatures is shown compassion from Heaven."

TALMUD: SHABBOS 151B

WHEN EVAN KALIK FOUNDED AND FUNDED THE CAT ADOPTION TEAM IN Sherwood, Oregon, there were two fundamental principles upon which he organized the combination cat shelter and adoption center. First, all C.A.T. cats were to remain C.A.T. cats. In other words, if an adopter found that, for one reason or another, they could no longer provide a loving home for their feline, that cat could be returned to the Cat Adoption Team, where every effort would be made to find it a new home. Second, the only circumstances under which a cat would be euthanized were if it suffered from a terminal illness, was beyond the capability of veterinary medicine to keep it alive and pain free, and was not eating. Then, and only then, would Evan reluctantly condone euthanizing the cat as the most compassionate and merciful way to end the animal's suffering.

Unfortunately, in the past several years, circumstances conspired to make it increasingly difficult for C.A.T. to honor those stipulations. As economic conditions worsened in the United States beginning in 2008, more and more adoptees began to return their kitties to C.A.T. The shelter was becoming crowded with returned cats, often the older animals for which it is always more challenging to find a home. Rumblings began to emanate from management that something would have to happen to lessen the "unwanted" cats being housed at the shelter. There were continual disagreements between the board of directors and the executive director (ED) about policy changes. Evan attempted to remove the ED but the board split over this decision, and eventually Evan (and I) were forced to resign. Since then, the president of the board has resigned, and the executive director left C.A.T. and was replaced by another person hired for that position. Evan

123

THE MAN WHO WOULDN'T KILL CATS

THE MAN WHO WOULDN'T KILL CATS

has not been informed as to any policy changes at C.A.T., but he fears that his criteria for maintaining a "no kill" shelter may have undergone revisions. We do not know, and have no contact with anyone at the shelter who will discuss the matter. Sadly, after spending millions of his own dollars to run the shelter, including the donation of the building and the construction of an onsite veterinary hospital, Evan has relinquished all association with the organization to which he devoted thirteen years of his life and a considerable portion of his personal fortune. It is for these reasons that Evan wishes to establish a new cat sanctuary.

The idea of a safe haven, a place of refuge and asylum – a sanctuary, in a word – is as old as the world itself. In Judaic tradition, it was the Israelite temple at Jerusalem, the holy of holies, and the tabernacle in which the Ark of the Covenant was enshrined during the wanderings of the Israelites. It evolved to mean a sacred building where fugitives were formerly entitled to immunity from arrest or execution, and eventually, a place protected by law where animals could live without interference. How appropriate that Evan Kalik, a Jew, would live to embody the combined meanings of the word.

Many of the cats that roam the land today are indeed fugitives, their only "crime" being that they have no safe haven, no holy of holies, no refuge or asylum. No sanctuary. Evan cannot change that for every homeless cast-away cat on the planet, but he does intend to build a sanctuary where the most outcast of the species within the Portland, Oregon, metropolitan area can, at last, find the peace that comes with the safety of sanctuary.

The sanctuary was originally conceived by Evan as a refuge for three groups of cats – those with FIV (feline AIDS), feral cats, and those with behavioral challenges, such as those who urinate inappropriately. "I've encountered so many situations of late, probably because of the economy, where people have to find another home for their cat immediately," says Evan. "I plan to work with my collaborators to set up a 'hot line' for such situations, and when they come to my attention, I will house those animals, as well, until we can find them a new home." There is no justification, from Evan's perspective, in euthanizing a cat because it has an illness it can live with, or because it has become an inconvenience or an economic burden. Evan cannot say "no" to a cat that can be treated. He has spent thousands of dollars on individual kitties, utilizing a variety of veterinary specialists.

"I know most people can't afford to do that," he says, "and it has become increasingly difficult for me to do so. At least with a sanctuary, I can consolidate their care, thereby saving their lives." Evan is delighted when the humans in the equation are positively affected by his efforts. If, on the other hand, the human involved is callous and cares not about the fate of the cat, he's just as pleased to do what he thinks right for the animal alone.

Yamhill County, Oregon, located to the southwest of Portland, and which includes the cities of McMinnville and Newberg, has no government-sponsored shelter and inadequate private non-profit facilities for handling the cat population of the area. Evan has offered to provide a fully equipped mobile vet hospital with an emphasis on the operation of a spay/neuter clinic that will serve the county's residents at varying locations and times every month. *We Care* (http://wecarefelinerescue.webs.com/), a feline rescue and adoption center in McMinnville, Oregon, will likely be one such location. *Homeward Bound* (http://www.adoptapet.com/adoption_rescue/78912.html), another shelter and adoption center in McMinnville, will also have the clinic parked at its location one weekend a month. Evan also envisions special spay/neuter clinics at various PetCo and PetSmart store locations around the area. "For those who have no or very limited resources," says Evan, "I want to offer spay/neuter services free of charge."

His caveat is that the county – or a donor – come up with the funds needed to hire a full-time veterinarian and two veterinary technicians. "At one time," says Evan, "I could afford to fund a project entirely whenever I saw the need. My remaining resources don't permit me to do that any longer. I need financial help from other like-minded animal lovers." The mobile clinic will remain at the sanctuary for one week each month to handle the medical needs of the feline residents. Because it is mobile, should emergencies arise at the sanctuary, the mobile clinic can return to serve the onsite needs of the cats anytime it is required. Nearby neighbors will also be offered the services of the clinic for their cats.

Then there is the need for two full-time employees to maintain operation of the sanctuary itself. To offset this expense, Evan plans to open a thrift store that will serve as an income generator for the sanctuary, while also providing room for an adoption outlet. "We'll have cats onsite who are ready for someone to provide them with a loving Forever Home," according to Evan. Here again, at least one full-time employee will be required to run this operation.

It is this dream into which Evan invites the reader's participation. In the process of creating a new 501c3 non-profit organization (working title: "Cat Alliance Team Sanctuary" or CATS), Evan needs contributions to breathe life into his plans for a cat sanctuary, mobile veterinary clinic, and thrift store. Even the smallest donations are welcomed, for they all add up to eventually bringing the dream into reality.

Send your tax-deductible contributions to:

The Cat Alliance Team Sanctuary (CATS)
P.O. Box 1482
Sherwood, Oregon, 97140

Email us at:
CatAllianceTeamSanctuary@4TheLoveOfCats.com